P9-DWA-091

DATE DUE

Let the Seller BEWARE!

Let the Seller BEWARE!

...

J. Elias Portnoy

The Complete Consumer Guide to
Getting Your Money's Worth

Collier Books / Macmillan Publishing Company · New York

Collier Macmillan Canada · Toronto

Maxwell Macmillan International
New York · Oxford · Singapore · Sydney

Collier Books
Macmillan Publishing Company
866 Third Avenue, New York, NY 10022

Collier Macmillan Canada, Inc.
1200 Eglinton Avenue East
Suite 200
Don Mills, Ontario M3C 3N1

Library of Congress Cataloging-in-Publication Data
Portnoy, J. Elias.
    Let the seller beware! : the complete consumer guide to getting
your money's worth / J. Elias Portnoy.
    p. cm.
Includes Index.
ISBN 0-02-036047-9
1. Consumer protection—United States.   2. Consumer educa-
tion—United States.   I. Title.
HC110.C63P67   1990
381.3'4'0973—dc20   90-46831   CIP

Macmillan books are available at special discounts for bulk purchases for sales promotions, premiums, fund-raising, or educational
use. For details, contact:
    Special Sales Director
    Macmillan Publishing Company
    866 Third Avenue
    New York, NY 10022

10 9 8 7 6 5 4 3 2 1

Printed in the United States of America

Contents

Preface

As you read this book, you will notice the absence of two words—words that appear all too often for most of our tastes. The words are—and try not to flinch—lawyer and complaint.

The reason why neither of these words make an appearance is because the purpose of this book is twofold: 1) to empower you to act on your own behalf without the need of a lawyer and 2) to keep you from feeling like you are making a complaint—you will simply feel like you are making those individuals and companies (meaning the sellers) who have entered into an agreement with you live up to their agreements and meet the expectations they have excited in you.

Acknowledgments

To my mother, Theo, who stood stalwartly beside me when the going was tough. To my father, Sy, who consistently and in a dignified fashion articulated the mainstream thinking that was my motivation. To my sister, Lois, for her continuous support and to my niece, Anna Lily, who represents the future world I hope I will influence in a positive way.

—J. ELIAS PORTNOY
March 11, 1990

1

■

Why I Became an Expert at Revenge

■

STATEMENT OF PHILOSOPHY

You pay for something expecting quality, but wind up with dreck. Duped and seduced, you almost feel like you've been the victim of a nonviolent crime, a con. You tell yourself, "From now on I'll be more careful," yet the bad experiences happen again and again. After you've been victimized and exploited, the question becomes: Should I do anything about it?

I personally answered the question by becoming an expert at revenge. But this did not just happen overnight. In fact, the story of how it happened can be compressed into a few unique experiences that span a period of nearly twenty years.

The story begins when I was all of four years old, at which time I began building models. Precisely fitting and gluing many dozens of small plastic pieces together made me very sensitive to the way things are constructed, and conscious of the effort it takes to make them right. The happiness I felt when I'd succeeded in producing a miniature replica of some dazzling machine—in most cases a car—was great. Not shy about advertising my accomplishments, I was like a miniature replica of Lee Iacocca.

And then it happened. I've blocked out the memory of the first time, but I know it happened quite often. What I'm referring to is that I'd come to a point in building a model when it would occur to me that no matter how much effort and ingenuity I summoned, I was not going to be able to complete it. The reason? Missing, broken, or improperly formed pieces. This was devastating. It was somewhat like taking a running jump on a broiling day into a swimming pool, only to find out, midair, that you'd been misled, the pool was drained. My—as it were—midair reaction included shock, fear, and a terrible sense of helplessness. Then I'd feel hurt and angry. I was not quiet about it. My parents whispered worriedly about temper tantrums. To me, screaming while stomping the partially built model into vacuum-sized bits was a perfectly natural ritual, a kind of war dance against invisible enemies.

Then, around the age of eight, I began getting an allowance. This introduced me to three magical concepts: My Own Money, Saving My Own Money, and Spending My Own Money. The effect was dynamic. The very next time I encountered a defect—I believe it was a cracked chassis in a classic Duesenberg—I very coolly gathered the pieces, put them back in the box, and set out for the toy store, confident that explaining the problem would result in a refund, a replacement, or because of my trouble, both. (I know we're warned not to count our chickens. I wasn't. I was counting emperor penguins.)

Now, along with certain memorable toys, nearly everyone has a cast of unforgettable childhood villains. There's the bogeyman, the neighborhood bully, the Wicked Witch of the West, your friend's mother who smacked you for crossing a street without looking. Well, in that nightmarish part of me reserved for hating, I'll always have a spot for the toy store salesman, who, responding to my polite and valid appeal, said, "How am I supposed to know you didn't break it yourself, sonny?"

The rebuke rocked me. Not knowing whether I was going to get mad or get angry, I stammered something about being honest, it's not fair, I didn't do anything wrong. The monster spoke again: "Look kid, I'm sorry, but whaddya expect for $3.50? Perfection? You want another one? Pay for it like everybody else." Such was my welcome to the wonderful wacky world of professional wrestling, otherwise known as customer service.

The next key experience took place years later. When my father decided to buy a new car, I went to work on him immediately. Because of my extensive knowledge in this area, I'd participated in the decision-making process on numerous occasions. But this time I didn't want to have just input, I was determined to exert my influence and persuade him to purchase a car that was much more expensive, not fashionable (yet), but clearly the class of the field.

I climbed way out on a limb and argued vehemently. The top-of-the-line quality of the automobile had so aroused my expectations that my enthusiasm proved contagious. The decision to buy was made; I awaited the delivery of Apollo's winged chariot with a mixture of excitement and anxiety.

The anxiety dissipated upon delivery. In construction, design, handling, and safety features, the vehicle was an obvious engineering triumph. The thud the doors made when I closed them was music to my ears. I played them like an instrument.

And then suddenly, heart-wrenchingly, the love affair was over. The wood veneer on the dashboard started peeling away;

the seams on the leather seats began separating; the rubber bushing in the underchassis started squeaking. Worst of all, the fuel injection system broke down repeatedly, leaving whoever was in the car stranded.

Did I take it personally? Not any more than, say, a swift kick in the pants. Feeling guilty and betrayed, hurt and outraged, I accompanied my parents time after time to the dealership. Many times I insisted on hanging around in the hopes that my urgent presence might motivate somebody to work on the car until it was really fixed.

Fat chance. Like the toy store salesman, the employees of the dealership treated us, particularly me, as if we were some kind of weird pesty perfectionists. "It's falling apart like an ancient sofa." Shrug, smile, snort. "You say the car broke down again where?" Shrug, smile, snort. I couldn't believe their indifference, their ridicule. Then, my very own father joined their camp, telling me to quit caring, leave well enough alone, as long as the damn thing gets us from point A to point B we should be happy.

The topper came—perhaps between fuel injection breakdown numbers four and five—with the publication of Philip Roth's novel *Portnoy's Complaint.* Wherever I went people used the coincidence of our names to display their wit: "Hey Portnoy, what's your complaint?" "I know you've gotta have complaints, Portnoy. Let's hear 'em." "Go ahead Portnoy, what're your complaints?" Needless to say, the comedians at the dealership had a blast.

It was depressing and humiliating. Meeting somebody I might just as well have said, "Hello, I'm Eli Laughingstock. Knock yourself out." For a while I began to withdraw. Being labeled a complainer, even if I hardly ever complained about anything, was not a source of popularity.

And then it dawned on me. I don't recall where I was, just that I felt instant elation. "My God," I thought, "I *do* have complaints. Yes I do. Tons of them. I hate the way our car has died. I can't stand the way those jerks at the dealership make us feel like it's our problem. It bothers me that our toaster burns the toast, our washing machine tends to flood, and our TV goes on the fritz."

When I voiced my thinking to my father, pointing out that maybe we should find out how to take positive action by taking our complaints directly to somebody in charge at the companies that apparently thought it was fine to sell us substandard products, or treat us like dogs, he said stuff like, "You can't fight city hall," and "Who needs unpleasantness?" and "It'll be a waste of time; besides, we'll drive ourselves crazy."

I knew this attitude was wrong. But all the people I talked to, including those of my own generation, agreed that the best path was the path of least resistance. Make adjustments, they more or less said, This Is Reality.

The opposition, plus plenty of bad experiences with products and services over the next years, served to crystallize my thinking. Years went by argumentatively. Then in my twenties I jumped on the fast track of corporate America, and began earning and spending a lot of money. Once again, Spending My Own Money triggered a further evolution: When I encountered a serious problem with a product or service, instead of just using it as ammunition to bolster my position, I actually did what I could to take action.

At first, my success ratio was zero. I had no idea what I was doing. Mainly, I managed to get into a wider variety of knuckle-whitening exchanges with an ever-expanding range of unhelpful company employees. My efforts also stirred up a chorus of sarcasm and skepticism from friends and relatives alike. "My son the big consumer fighter," my father would say with a shake of his head and a sigh.

But I swallowed my pride and persisted. I knew I had embarked on a learning experience, and regarded each failure as a kind of laboratory experiment on which I kept very detailed notes. Gradually, I fine-tuned my approach. Here and there I even got a positive resolve. The successes were even more instructive than the failures. My ratio soared.

As the news got around, the chorus changed its tune. Pest, nut, complainer, fanatic turned into, "I was wondering . . . I've got a minor problem . . . would you see what you can do? Don't go to any trouble though." I loved it and never turned down a case, which simply enabled me to get a greater breadth of experience faster. The word was out; the circle of people asking for assistance grew and spread. Otherwise highly intelligent, successful, energetic, and usually reserved acquaintances would take me aside and describe how angry and exploited they felt. Would I give them a hand?

Besides the fact that I was becoming overloaded, I realized the time had come to document my knowledge when a fellow who I really didn't like prevailed upon me to get his money back for a trip he'd taken to the Orient.

No sooner had I complied than I set to work to create this action guide, intent on conveying everything I know in a manner that will stimulate you to enjoy the pleasure of not only acting on your own behalf, but getting what you deserve.

2.

The Brick Wall and
the Corporate Shell

■

STATEMENT OF PHILOSOPHY

Statistics show that one out of four purchases causes
legitimate grounds for dissatisfaction, yet at least 70
percent of us never make a peep when we encounter
a problem. Why? Because most of us have ideas and
perceptions and fears which prevent us from taking action. In addition to these personal brick walls, most of
us don't know how to cope with the very real shells
that corporations build to protect themselves. Together, the brick walls and corporate shells succeed in
stymieing the overwhelming majority of American consumers.

• A young woman realized she had been overcharged by her
local telephone company to the tune of two hundred dollars.

As best she could determine, the calls were made during the day when she was at work—presumably by her pet cat. Though concerned about the overcharge, she was even more concerned that persistent effort on her part to resolve the problem might create worse problems. Specifically, if she withheld payment on the amount in dispute, the phone company could cut off her service, then tack on a reconnection fee if she failed to win her point. She also worried about having to pay a large security deposit, while at the same time losing her good credit rating. The sum total of her fears was greater than the money, so she paid the overcharge.

• An elderly widower on a fixed income bought a new stove. When the thermostat proved wildly inaccurate, thus ruining a succession of roasts, the senior citizen called the retailer. The retailer told him to call the manufacturer, which he did. After being transferred from person to person inside the company, he was finally told by someone in the service department that they were not in a position to help, but he could expect to be called back soon. The call never came. He tried again, was again bounced around, but this time wound up with an employee who claimed they did not have the proper paperwork. Again the promise of a call back was made but not kept. After a third round of similar futility, the senior citizen decided it was not worth getting demoralized over, so he experimented until he could work the stove without an accurate thermostat.

• A middle-aged bachelor's pride and joy, an expensive European car, got a huge dent while parked in his garage. The bachelor approached the garage attendants, who denied any knowledge. When pressed, they became defensive, then abusive. Holding his temper, the bachelor did get the name and number of the garage's owner. The owner turned out to be a real prince—after denying any responsibility, he actually issued sly threats about potential future damages. The bachelor seethed. There were no other conveniently located garages, and he was afraid the situation could escalate out of control. So, swallowing his pride, he shelled out for the repair, apologized to the owner, and gave the attendants a few extra bucks.

• A young upwardly mobile professional couple had the bedroom of their co-op redone. For whatever reasons, glaring mistakes were made: The bed was slightly lopsided on its platform; certain drawers underneath the bed could not be opened and closed without strain and scraping; from some angles the built-in lighting was blindingly bright. After wrangling with the subcontractor, who passed the fault onto the interior decorator, they wrangled with the interior decorator, who passed the fault back onto the subcontractor. Their lawyer advised them that legal action was possible, but in the end they decided the matter wasn't worth their time and effort.

These experiences are typical. After all, 70 percent of you, the American consumer, never take action when you encounter a faulty product or poor service. Instead, you come up against a brick wall, that intangible force that keeps you from taking action. Then you back off, pay erroneous bills, throw out defective merchandise, do your best to cavalierly ignore incompetence, rudeness, and false promises. So formidable does the brick wall seem that you would rather suffer in silence than probe it, check it out, test its reality.

This obstacle would not exist if the majority of businesses treated you with respect and consideration, gave you even more than you expected, and in general, made the experience of dealing with them as easy and mutually satisfying as possible. But such companies are maddeningly rare. Far more common are companies that act, in effect, as if your gain is somehow their loss.

So the brick wall does exist—if primarily in the mind. Not as a single, formidable obstacle, but as many different things to many different people. The brick wall is a metaphor for whatever reason or combination of reasons cause you, the overwhelming majority of consumers, to recoil from the objective of obtaining what you are entitled to from companies. Let's take a look at those reasons that seem so very real and so very compelling. The idea here is for you to identify yourself by recognizing the reason or reasons that constitute your own particular brick wall. Then we can begin to go about the business of tearing the walls down.

Brick Wall #1: "If I wanted to do something about a problem, I wouldn't know where or how to begin."

In the first place, the marketplace is vast, complex, and disorienting. There are dozens of varieties of everything, but very little guidance. When faced with a problem, many consumers would simply rather switch brands than think about where or how to raise an objection. This reason is mentioned especially by older consumers who grew up in a much less daunting, more trustworthy, and more intimate consumer environment. As one elderly woman put it: "I guess I won't ever get used to the way things have become. Sometimes, it seems as if it happened overnight. And I can't quite get my bearings."

Along with slipping standards in goods and services, there is a different, more charged, more aggressive interpersonal climate. A man in his midfifties said, "Everybody is in such a hurry. Not just young people, everybody. I'm afraid that if I did go up to somebody and try to explain, they'd act like they couldn't be bothered. Why had I picked on them, anyway?" This may sound like the Sunday-driver crowd, but it isn't. Plenty of very savvy individuals will go blank if pressed on the issue of expressing their dissatisfaction. "Look, I've already got enough to think about without thinking about that, okay?" is a familiar response. "As far as I'm concerned," said one man in late middle age, who was extremely active in many spheres, "asking me how I'd go about getting what was, or should be, coming to me, is like asking me to look for a tablet in the woods that had some unknown writing on it. Even if I did find it, then I'd have to translate the thing."

Brick Wall #2: "It isn't worth my time."

For many consumers, life is lived at one hundred miles an hour. Setting priorities is by no means easy. There are schedules, appointments, agendas. Finding time for what seems to matter most requires careful budgeting. This reason is cited with great frequency by young professionals who are upwardly mobile, upscale targets for every sales pitch. Said one harried guy in finance, "I'm on a fast track. Sure it annoys the hell out of me when I pay for some piece of crap, but trying to do something about it would feel like I was going in reverse since I probably wouldn't get what I was after anyway."

Having come a long way in a short time, these people are acutely aware of how much can be accomplished and how much can be earned in brief time frames. No group is more disgusted or more bitter about the inferior quality of so many of their consumer experiences, and when they have somebody in front of them at whom they can vent their spleen, they do. But they don't expect real results. They think they'll run faster in the future, work harder, earn more, put their grievances behind them, always behind them. "Some of the junk I pay for actually starts to make me a little sick," said a fast-rising young woman in finance, "but like everything else, you've got to calculate the trade-off. If I thought I had a good shot at sticking it to some of these junk sellers, you better believe I would."

Brick Wall #3: "It's just not worth the effort."

Consumers of every stripe and description cite this reason. They talk about how busy they are. How draining their lives have become. They often refer to themselves as survivors: Life is tough but so are they. "I've only got so much energy," said a nuclear-powered mother of three. "I've got to be aware of how I parcel it out, otherwise I'll find myself flat on my face and wonder how I got there." The feeling here is that the wisest course of action is to put your energy and effort where the outcome is most predictable. There is nothing lazy, irresponsible, or indifferent about this attitude. They feel that life is constantly coming at them and it's all they can do to stay afloat. Said one affluent mother: "Sometimes I get so mad when something breaks or doesn't work right that I have to restrain myself from taking it out on the wrong people. Like my kids. Sometimes I think it probably costs me more effort to control myself than it would to give the people who deserve it a piece of my mind." Undoubtedly, she is right. Another aspect of this attitude was voiced by a man to a tableful of agreeing diners: "You know the expression, 'Don't throw good money after bad'? Well, I say, don't throw good effort and good energy after misspent money. Otherwise the damn problem is given a sort of second life. It gets to linger. I say cut your losses."

Brick Wall #4: "I don't believe any good would come of taking action anyway."

This reason is inherent in each of the reasons stated already. If you play out the string a little bit with almost all silent sufferers, they'll eventually get around to describing their underlying sense of futility. Even if they did have a strategy for getting even, they feel it would be negated by the stubborn, combative nature of companies themselves. (Much more on this later.) Said one man, a self-described go-getter: "What's the point of going after something you're not going to get?" Said another fellow: "Do I seem like a guy who enjoys banging his head against a wall?" Individuals who list this as the first reason that comes to mind tend to think of themselves as skeptics, realists. They work hard at not being disappointed, at not expecting too much. "I don't for a New York second doubt my ability to get most things done," said a thirtyish woman who could clearly handle herself. "But I'm realistic. If it looks like a crash-and-burn situation, I back off."

Brick Wall #5: "In the first place I don't expect high quality."

This reason is given by an astonishing number of consumers under the age of twenty. Substandard, mediocre experiences are all they've ever known. The disposable quality of so many products is not exactly news to them. Lousy service is what they've been weaned on. Ambiguous morality, a culture that prizes immediate gratification and treats life almost as if it's mere entertainment—these are the conditions they've known.

Said one young man with considerable consumer experience under his stressed leather jacket: "You know the scene in *Back to the Future* [Part I] where Michael J. Fox walked past that Fifties gas station and all those happy, neatly pressed dudes rushed around servicing that car like they were a pit crew? Me and my friends cracked up at the time. But later we talked about how nice it must have been back then."

Brick Wall #6: "I like to give companies the
same benefit of the doubt I do people."

The gentle generous souls who run into this brick wall tend to
be keenly conscious of their own shortcomings. "I know how
hard it is to do things right all the time," said one elderly
woman who appeared to be someone who came pretty close.
"If I was going to hold anybody up to high standards, it would
be myself, first and last." Not that this reason is by any means
limited to candidates for sainthood. In fact, the reason runs,
perhaps a little deeper, through the entire consumer population. Wanting to give companies the benefit of the doubt
reflects the desire to keep the buyer/seller relationship as im-
personal and abstract as possible.

Said one super-functioning mother/daycare center administrator: "If I thought for a second companies were making a
calculated attempt to sell us stuff that they could improve on
without going out of business, I'd consider it a personal affront.
I like to think they're doing the best they can in a very competitive atmosphere." The world and the people in it are seen as
being spectacularly imperfect; inadequate products and services are only a natural, inevitable reflection of that imperfec-
tion.

Brick Wall #7: "If I was more careful and
really paid attention to what I was doing, I
wouldn't get stuck with bad stuff."

Quite a lot of consumers turn the experience of being taken
advantage of and mistreated back onto themselves. Indeed, for
those with a penchant for self-deprecation, the act of consuming is a real gold mine. Confirmation of a person's negative
feelings about themselves can be located without a map and a

compass. "It's my fault for not reading up or asking around," said a woman who had had a series of bad experiences with nonperforming appliances. Blaming oneself for consumer experiences that do not live up to snuff is also a way of regaining control. Speaking about a Barcalounger that had broken after two weeks of use, a man who would have to be described as almost obsessively cautious said, "I'm definitely not impulsive or impetuous or anything like that. Still, it serves me right because once I found a store that promised fast delivery, I stopped looking seriously. If I hadn't been shortsighted the problem would never have arisen." Consumers who cite this as their personal brick wall tend to use the expression "the story of my life" quite often. And although thankful, they tend to be less appreciative and jubilant than most when shown how easy it really is to resolve problems.

Brick Wall #8: "I don't want to get into a confrontation."

This is the first of the powerful personal fears expressed by such a large percentage of consumers. As with all fears, it has at least part of its origin in early experience. In other words, from the outset of their lives, many people have the experience of seeing how defensively, angrily, and even abusively others react to criticism or faultfinding. Thus, fear of getting into a confrontation with a company is, in part, an extension or outgrowth of the experience people have had with personal relations.

"Like they kept saying in *The Godfather*, 'It's not personal, it's business,'" said one veteran consumer. "And I know that's the only attitude to take when you're getting what you should get from a company. But I can't help thinking I'm going to wind up like somebody in the movie. You know, a stiff." The gentleman is absolutely right—it's not personal, it's business.

Yet the unpleasantness of confrontation makes it hard not to dwell on. "I know transactions aren't supposed to be personal," said a young man, "but once you start calling attention to something you don't like or you think is unfair, it starts to feel personal in a hurry." As reminiscent of difficult and frightening experience as dealing with companies may be, such dealings, in point of fact, occupy an entirely different realm.

Another consumer, a man with a considerable amount of money and a bankful of consumer horror stories, said, "I willingly go the long way around the block to avoid confrontation with a business. I'm afraid that if I get into it with some poor slob company representative, they'll do what comes naturally and there'll be fireworks. Then the incident will prey on my mind for weeks, and who needs that? Besides, I won't win." The anticipation of confrontation is not some wild fantasy; too many companies do all they can to foster this anticipation, this fear.

Brick Wall #9: "I'm afraid things will escalate and get completely out of control."

This may seem like a rewording of Brick Wall #8, but it's actually cited by a different group of consumers. The majority of these consumers grew up on conflict. They readily argue and engage in interpersonal battles. Angry and always ready to raise the stakes, to throw fuel on the fire themselves, they expect others, including companies, to do the same. Psychologists tell us that these people tend to ascribe qualities they possess to others. "I think about getting even with companies that sell me bunk," said a short-fused Wall-Streeter. "Then I think how the company will retaliate. Who knows what they might do to me? And I've got too much to lose." The notion that a company has an arsenal of weapons at its disposal to unleash on a persistent justice-seeking consumer is hardly discouraged by quite a few companies. Though very compelling, the fear that a company will actually go out of its way to retaliate, to hurt an individual consumer, is irrational. (Companies do not go after consumers. In fact, as we shall see, companies are deathly afraid of consumers, and if approached in the appropriate manner, will bend over backward to appease and placate.)

Much more rational is the fear that a face-to-face confrontation with a company employee, say a salesperson or department manager, will escalate into an out-of-control situation. "I have visions of going into a store to buy gloves and winding up on the floor wrestling around with some horrible, rude salesperson," said a successful young woman.

Brick Wall #10:   "I'm afraid of getting humiliated."

Like the previous fears, this one runs so deep in people that they anticipate it even in situations where the likelihood of occurrence is slim to none. Take the woman who did extremely well in the "dog-eat-dog" world of commercial real estate: "As long as I'm the seller I feel like I'm in control, on top, and nothing bad is going to happen. When I'm the buyer, however, I'm on the defensive. Years ago I tried to get a refund for a movie because the movie reel kept breaking. The theater manager and I ended up in the lobby screaming at each other. Then, in front of what seemed like the entire human race, he told me I was a spoiled, obnoxious jerk. I quit saying anything and nearly died of embarrassment. Ever since then, when I'm unhappy with something I've paid for, it's almost as if I'm transported back to that lobby. Boy, does that keep my mouth shut."

This woman's experience speaks for so many consumers:

They've been the victim of a bad deal, tried to address the problem without knowing how to, felt humiliated in some way or another, and been gun-shy ever since. The general feeling is that it's bad enough to have been cheated or misled, why compound the misfortune? Humiliation is one of the most painful and feared human experiences. The chances of being humiliated are greatest in situations where one feels uncertain and overmatched—which is precisely how the majority of consumers feel when they consider the possibility of forcing a company to provide them with what they're entitled to.

These are the top-ten brick walls cited by consumers. Each one is thought to have sufficient stopping power. Taken en masse, they might seem to present an unconquerable obstacle. But do they really? Do they possess any reality outside the minds of consumers?

The answer to this question is yes . . . and no . . . no and yes. The truth is that the mortar that keeps all these brick walls from falling down is made up of two basic elements. The first has to do with the fact that consumers simply do not know how to approach companies in a way that virtually guarantees them success. If you don't know how to get results, and think there is no chance your helter-skelter approach will have a favorable outcome, why in heaven's name would you bother? You wouldn't. Unless you happen to be either a masochist or one of those people who temperamentally don't let a matter drop until they've exhausted whatever means of resolve they have at their disposal.

The second element has to do with the fact that a vast number of companies enclose themselves in a shell that offers a great deal of very real resistance to any consumer who has a problem. To be sure, there are dozens of companies toiling zealously to provide excellent design, craftsmanship, and customer relations, but the majority of them aren't. Quite the contrary. Because of the basic structure of most corporations, what they provide is less than satisfactory. Rather than upgrading or undergoing top-to-bottom restructuring, they act to preserve themselves by hiding inside what they think is a protective shell. Companies that open themselves wide to consumers—like Nordstroms, Federal Express, Robert Krupps Appliances, and Ghurka Luggage, to name just a few—are experiencing fantastic success, which just goes to show how self-undermining corporate shells really are.

Most consumers expect companies to be combative, which is why they create reasons—i.e., brick walls—to rationalize their lack of action. Anyone who knows how to penetrate the shell quickly and easily and effectively has no rhyme or reason for a brick wall.

Before we look on the other side of the shell, before we zap the brick walls and make them disappear, let's take a look at the different kinds of shells so many companies imagine they can't do without.

1. *The game is Ping-Pong and you're the ball.* . . . Many companies make it very hard on you to determine who is to blame for your problem. Is it the wholesaler, the retailer, or the manufacturer? They send you bouncing back and forth in what comes to seem like an endless rally until you're so beat up that you give up.

2. *You can run but they can hide.* . . . A lot of companies are difficult to locate. Needless to say, communicating with a company by mail or phone is a bit of a problem if you have no idea where it is. Hiring a private detective is a might costly. Then, when you do manage to locate the company, they don't have an 800 number and so must be called long-distance at your expense. Letters are simply not acknowledged.

3. *Seek, find, so what.* . . . The company does not provide any type of customer service or consumer relations department.

When you do call you get shuffled around aimlessly, put on hold, and kept on hold. Time does not exactly fly by when you're on hold. And writing meets with no response.

4. *I've been disconnected twice already. . . .* Company operators deliberately disconnect problematic callers. You call back, get a different operator, are forced to tell your story from the beginning, only to get disconnected in the middle again. This is not good for either the well-being of your heart or your mind.

5. *As low person on the totem pole, I suggest you dry up.* . . . Companies spend little time training and motivating their front-line people, which hurts their morale and often causes them to be unhelpful, if not downright hostile. Rather than dealing with your problem, you wind up hating the person you're dealing with.

6. *The new robots. . . .* Some customer relations employees are trained to be virtual robots. Considering the variety of your requests and grievances, the standardized responses you get are not very likely to be of use. Furthermore, though perhaps well trained in the technical aspects of their jobs, these employees have no preparation for handling different sorts of people.

7. *The big runaround. . . .* You are misdirected again and again to the wrong section of the company and find yourself talking to employees who insist they aren't authorized to make a decision about your problem—this after you've talked to them longer than you've spoken to, say, your spouse in a month.

8. *The run aground. . . .* Another variation of the runaround. Here you're told that the person who can help you is absent, unavailable, or perpetually on another line. Attempts to reach them by letter are infuriatingly responded to with a polite note suggesting that you try calling again.

9. *It's your fault, stupid. . . .* This is a particularly vexing as well as common variety of shell. "You didn't read the directions properly," says someone who makes you think you've died and gone to hell. "No doubt you're mishandling the product" is another good one. "You're probably misusing the product," "We've never had a complaint like this before," "I'm sure there's nothing wrong with the product," . . . and on and on.

10. *Stonewalling. . . .* This technique of customer disservice sounds like "I'm sorry, but there's nothing we can do about a problem such as yours," or "That's our policy and that's really all there is to say," or "I suggest if you feel you must pursue the matter, take it up with the store where you made the purchase," or "If the company submitted to each and every complaint, we wouldn't be in business very long now would we?" etc., etc.

11. *It's as if you'd never opened your mouth. . . .* Companies respond to your call or letter by sending a standardized return letter that ignores the issue entirely while patronizingly thanking you for your interest in their company.

12. *The sleeper-hold. . . .* The company lulls you to sleep by expressing eager interest in resolving your problem, makes all kinds of promises about follow-up, then files the entire matter into the wastebasket.

13. *If you are Odysseus or own a supercomputer. . . .* The company outlines a course of action for you to take that is so strenuous and so complicated that it thwarts you from pursuing resolve.

Chances are you have experienced at least one and probably more of these ways in which companies deter you from getting what you are entitled to. Whether your reaction was to go into a blind rage, lose your voice, and stomp around, or whether you simply took the whole situation lying down and justified it as part of the price of doing business in a consumer society, you've had a little something taken out of you; they chipped away at your pocketbook, your pride, and your sense of fairness. Now, turn the page and see how to deal with the problems that arise. Turn your bad experiences around, take negative energy and make it positive. In short, generate good triumphant feelings while earning financial rewards.

3.

Piercing the
Corporate Shell

■

STATEMENT OF PHILOSOPHY

The frightfully complex inner structure of most companies has two intentions: to protect executives at different levels from each other; and to protect everyone
from outsiders—i.e., you. Companies hide inside different shells, which are like defense mechanisms, because
it is they who are afraid and vulnerable.

• An executive with a consumer products company described a business cycle that is revealing of the way many
corporations operate. He told of how a particular product
gained a major share of the market. Because top management
wanted to cash in as much as possible, the price of the product
was raised. Then, to justify a second raise, cosmetic changes in
the product were made. Consumers clearly considered the

price hikes to be baseless as they switched to other brands in droves. For a time, however, the high cost per unit kept profits up. But eventually, sales dipped to a point where the bottom line was being very negatively affected. Rather than reinvesting money to make changes that would justify the product's high cost, management adopted other cost-cutting measures (like large-scale layoffs). Finally, a new management team was brought in. The new team shifted its focus to a different product, and the cycle began anew.

• A marketing group for a multinational corporation was asked to develop a promotional program to increase the visibility of a particular product by offering consumers some form of reward. The group came up with an innovative concept that they agreed would be very exciting for consumers. The manager overseeing the group supposedly took the concept and pitched it to top management. He came back saying that the idea had been rejected in favor of another promotion that was exactly in keeping with the lackluster ideas of the past. Sometime later, quite by accident, a member of the marketing team learned that their manager had never even mentioned the concept to any of his superiors. On his own he had decided that the innovative quality of the concept might be perceived as controversial, and that if he was identified with something controversial, he could be regarded as unsuited for future advancement. In just this manner do many of the best consumer-oriented ideas get stifled.

• Product improvements are few and far between. Most pet projects of junior-level managers are never taken into serious consideration, while those of ultraconservative, supercautious senior managers are usually rather insignificant. A top-level manager related a story that illustrates this perfectly. As a junior-level manager he came up with a wonderful idea that had the potential of improving consumer satisfaction with a certain product and, simultaneously, increasing the product's price/value relationship. He excitedly took the idea to the research and development facility, expecting to create a bit of a sensation. Instead, person after person told him to go back to his office and figure out a way to "remarket" what they already had. "New" ideas—even those based on consumer feedback—would most likely ruffle feathers and possibly cost people their jobs.

The issue of business review documents illustrates in microcosm a lot that is wrong with corporations. These voluminous documents, which frequently occupy dozens of lower- and middle-level executives for as much as one-fifth of the working year, are meant to summarize the opportunities the business faces and to identify the problem areas. The dinosaur documents break down the performance of each product or service by offering an overwhelming multitude of numerical analyses. Since everyone is 100 percent determined to keep things looking healthy until they're promoted, the numbers are manipulated to produce only favorable conclusions. Thus, aspiring managers are protected from inspection by senior managers. What's more, senior managers who have, after all, been there before know that the documents are created to obscure and so insist on ten-page executive summaries. Each year there is much talk about abridging the format, yet because the documents are one of those institutionalized methods by which large numbers of people are protected from critical scrutiny, they continue to be written, year after year.

All companies concentrate on projecting a good image. They want to be perceived as providing quality products or services. They want to be thought of as being responsive to consumers and retailers; as being willing to spend whatever money and energy is necessary to continuously upgrade what they're selling; as being good to work for; as being upstanding citizens of the community, which, depending upon their size, might mean good citizens of the planet.

Quite recently a few major American companies have taken well-publicized looks at themselves. Horrified at what they found, they underwent top-to-bottom restructuring. They streamlined and simplified their operations, they began to wage an all-out campaign for quality and customer satisfaction, and instead of merely paying lip service to various moral commitments, they acted to turn their images into reality. Such companies are to be highly commended; what they did was to their credit (and profitability). But it should be noted that in virtually every case where a company underwent a painstaking reassessment, it did so because it had to. These companies were in serious trouble; they had not only lost their once mighty position, but many were in jeopardy of being squeezed out or eliminated from the marketplace altogether. So they dissolved their corporate shells, and now, having nothing to hide, are easy for consumers to deal with.

But beware!!! Flying the quality banner, flying the customer service banner is very much in vogue. Upward of 80 percent of the largest American corporations have—with considerable fanfare—expanded their quality-enhancement programs, and are dropping serious coin on advertisements that proclaim they are number one in customer service. (There are so many self-proclaimed number ones out there, maybe they should have some sort of play-off.)

Sadly, however, what the vast majority of these companies are doing is nothing but hype. The lip service they pay to quality and customer service is a reaction to the fact that the overwhelming majority of consumers have indicated in surveys that quality, durability, and customer service are much more important to them than price or appearance. As trend-alert as companies are, they're perfectly willing to spend loads of money proclaiming their new attitude and behavior. However, real substantive change and real improvement are a rarity.

The companies that are actually determined to make quality and customer service their first priorities are open and forthright. Their managers are preconditioned to foster contact with consumers in an effort to make doing business a mutually beneficial dynamic. Efficient and honestly self-critical on the inside, they are well disposed to outsiders—i.e., consumers. However, the managers of companies that are poorly run, bloated and devious, vulnerable and retreative, continue to regard the world outside them with harsh, contemptuous, and cynical eyes. These managers look upon the population of consumers as targets, as stupid insensitive targets, who wouldn't know the difference between a cost-saving change and a real product improvement if they fell over it. The way they look at consumers is not unlike the way a con artist regards the suckers he's fleecing. The typical managerial attitude is cut a corner, eliminate an amenity, make some meaningless alteration in the packaging or graphics—the sheeplike consumers will go along with anything as long as they don't realize what's really happening, as long as they get stroked with nice words and associations. Managers of such companies who resist this insidious attitude by making waves internally or blowing the whistle publicly are routinely fired. Thus, there is nobody to object to the kinds of comments one hears at meetings between like-minded managers who are "in it" together: "Hey, nobody will notice the difference and we'll save X thousands"; "We've gotta figure some way to minimize the damages to our public perception by getting a positive message across"; "Those new colors on the package tested better, I think it'll stand a price hike"; "I don't care if you do it as long as it boosts sales"; "If the media gets hold of this, we're dead"; "We've had a few complaints, but if we handle them right, they won't become a problem." Etc., etc., ad nauseam.

Why all the hostility? What's with all the defensiveness? The obvious answer is that companies know they're guilty of mismanagement; they're aware of their failure to provide what they promise. They're like a person who cannot take responsibility for his behavior, but must locate blame elsewhere. Unwilling to find fault with themselves, they find fault with everybody around them. The managers in these companies develop self-serving rationalizations that serve to make them feel superior while diminishing the dignity of the people outside the corporation.

The reasons for these attitudes and the reason why it's so difficult for corporations to change their attitudes and their way of doing business lie in the way so many of them are structured. In effect, the problems they cause consumers are really a reflection of the problems executives have with each other. Of course, the companies we're concerned with have somewhat different structures, management layouts, and stated business philosophies. Yet they also have a lot in common. So speaking very generally, let's pierce the corporate shell and take a peek at the generic corporate reality inside. Once you see the strange anatomy of a typical corporation, you'll have an idea why they're so self-protective and combative, and realize how vulnerable and scared they are. Then your brick walls—those rationalizations for doing nothing in the face of all those corporate shells—won't seem so real, and you'll be primed for learning how to get revenge, get even, and get what you're entitled to.

To begin with, corporations are shaped like pyramids—or, perhaps more accurately, like walruses, blubbery from the neck down. In any event, the room at the top is very, very small, while the egos trying to get in are very, very fat. Everyone is vying for the top spots. Senior management is egocentric and greed-driven. In recent times, as top executives have become the new superstars, acquiring fabulous wealth, hobnobbing with the glitterati, divorcing then remarrying beautiful women half their age (so-called Trophy Wives), the desirability (and therefore the status and power) of reaching the top has become, if anything, even greater than ever before. Is it any wonder that, considering these circumstances, top management is not exactly in any rush to make full-scale revamping their genuine priority? Unless they're pressed, unless they're forced to take aggressive action, they have every reason to preserve the status quo that has been so very, very good to them.

In order to take what they so obscenely and unabashedly take, top management has needed to create a mystique about itself, a mystique based, in part, on separateness and inaccessibility. Today's top managers maintain as great a distance from the players below them as possible. They work to be seen as larger than life, mythic, deserving. With power over everyone, and contact with almost no one (except others at their level), they look down from their airy perch and rationalize: Since the buck stops here, I deserve a baronial life-style; the little people just waste my valuable time; those below me are too small-minded to see the "big picture." Distanced and disdainful of their own people, imagine how cynical they are about the needs and entitlement of common ordinary consumers.

Below these self-glorifying upper echelons, things get really messy. It is here that companies begin to resemble giant mazes or governmentlike bureaucracies. It is here in the bloated, blubbery middle, composed of tiers upon tiers of middle managers, that rampant inefficiency and disregard for the reality of what's being sold flourish. It is here where a majority of consumer problems can be resolved. It is here where you frequently get revenge.

In the meantime, before we find out how, it's important to characterize this unruly world and the middle managers who occupy it.

Middle managers want more money, more power, more job security. They want increased authority over each other; they want promotions, pay raises, and big quarterly bonuses. Possessing mostly mediocre skills and capabilities, they are well aware that any increase of any kind makes them more entrenched, less likely to be lopped off when cutbacks become necessary. They get constant pressure from senior management above them, and feel constant pressure from the junior players below, who are seeking to displace them. The nature of their position makes them insecure, suspicious, competitive, self-protective, and self-justifying. It is in their interest to make what they do as abstruse, as seemingly important but as nonduplicative as possible. Sometimes it appears as if their actual job is to remain as squeaky clean as a new penny. They recoil from associating with any business idea or decision that might be considered controversial. Since change is always controversial, change is their nemesis. Independence, individualism, and creative spiritedness are not generally found in these ranks.

Middle managers are adaptive, like protoplasm that seeks warm, safe things to glom on to. Self-interested and self-seeking above all else, they try to pull off the trick of appearing nonthreatening yet indispensable. As a bunch of bandwagon riders, they expend their energies trying to hold their position and almost invisibly edge forward. Along the way they focus on the kind of short-term, stopgap measures that are meant to keep things looking healthy, regardless of consumer disenchantment.

Being risk-averse, these corporate players avoid interaction with consumers at all costs. Unless a company has explicitly outlined consumer-oriented policies, these players feel that dealing with consumers puts them in the position of having a lot to lose and little to gain. They're in a bind. They think: If I handle the problem, maybe senior management will come down on me because taking the problem seriously means we are admitting that a problem exists; on the other hand, if I don't handle the problem, maybe the feared and despised consumer will somehow manage to go over my head, and I'll get hammered for not protecting one of my bosses. (In articles and interviews, a number of managers have complained that giving them the responsibility for executing and managing the success of a product or service, while withholding sufficient authority to resolve problems as they see fit, puts them in an untenable position.)

Senior managers protect themselves from middle managers; middle managers protect themselves from senior managers and from each other; junior, entry-level managers protect themselves from those at the same level and those above them. The focus is not on product, innovation, improvement, or customer satisfaction; the real and abiding focus of most corporate players is on internal politics, the brutal infighting out of which some players are assured of moving quietly up the ladder. Ruffle feathers, suggest a new way of doing business, attempt to accomplish something that raises the standards, and you're likely to find yourself dead in the water, or worse, terminated. The message that radiates throughout the corporation is: Be good, be quiet, worry about yourself, take care, cover your tracks by making what you do seem impenetrable and incomprehensible; be prepared at all times to dodge, duck, get out of the way of a hit that might come from any direction at any time.

What makes the world of all these managers even stranger is that they are all organized into fiefdoms, strongholds. Every senior manager has a team of midlevel players who are loyal to them, trying to make them look good, protecting their territory from competitive raids by other teams. This simultaneously insulates the individual player from critical scutiny, and intensifies their competitive fervor as they form alliances with the fiefdom. There are so many strange contradictions here. Be a total team player, but distinguish yourself somehow for promotion. Be nonthreatening, noncontroversial, attract as little attention as possible, yet somehow reveal your ambitiousness, competitiveness, and competence. The impossibly complex reporting systems, the hierarchies within hierarchies, the paralyzingly mixed signals have very distinct advantages for everybody except the consumer: They keep players locked into their little battles so they pose almost no threat to senior management; and they enable countless numbers of high-paid lackeys to dig in to a kind of nervous obscurity from where they can continue to cash in a paycheck and rake in a sweet bonus.

Considering how confusing, misleading, demoralizing, scary, and intimidating most corporations are to the very people who work in them, is it any surprise that the overwhelming majority of consumers are unwilling or afraid to get involved in pursuing their entitlement? But the truth is that corporate players are easily motivated. Jump-starting them to give you resolve or at least guide you through the maze is easily done. For in the beginning and in the end, they are human beings, susceptible to the right pressures, available for service to anyone who understands their position or predicament. Perhaps one way to further bring them down to size is to introduce you to a typical fiefdom. The makeup of this representative team is drawn from a combination of personal experience and conversations with executives from an assortment of middle- to large-sized corporations. Each player might be male or female, young or not-so-young.

So please meet:

- *The I-Got-More-Fries-with-My-Burger Type.* This player sits in your office counting the number of ceiling tiles so as to be able to compare them to the number in his office. This obsessively competitive player competes with everyone about everything—except about doing a good job.

- *The Solid Dependable Teammate.* This real team player has never ruffled a feather, and always, always plays it safe. She wouldn't go out on a limb to rescue a baby. Considered loyal, trustworthy, restrained, and controlled. A safe bet to go far in the corporation, but never all the way to the top.

- *The Scapegoat.* Lack of any discernible intelligence gets this player in trouble frequently. Not sharp enough to deflect hits, he has difficulty completing basic tasks. Swifter, shrewder players use this person as an excuse when the going gets hot and heavy. The perfect person to point the finger at, their resumé usually lists an impressive number of employers.

- *The Maverick.* Very sharp and smart and wants everyone to know it. Tries to accomplish a good deal in an environment where moving paper clips from one side of the desk to the other is looked upon as a promotable activity. Has fine ideas and immense energy, but eventually gets eaten up in power struggles. An independent and emotional type who ultimately opts for entrepreneurial life, she is the one player who will resolve a consumer's problem without thinking twice about it.

- *The Snake.* Pretends to be everybody's friend and confidant. However, he uses whatever personal information he can gather to burn others and aggrandize himself. Though he produces little or no meaningful work, he is valuable to management because it is like having a snitch on the inside.

- *Proof of the Peter Principle.* A player who was good at the lower levels, but reached her level of radical incompetence at, say, the entry VP level. To handle failure this player often turns to alcohol or substance abuse, which causes her to make substantial trouble. Because this player has usually been brought along under the protective wing of a very senior player, she lasts longer than she should, then tends to be able to move laterally from company to company.

- *The Golden One.*   A very good player who knows how to play the game. Capable of moving business forward without ruffling feathers, deals well with all levels of employees, and earns widespread respect. A rare bird, who a lot of players try to attach themselves to, this player goes right to the top unless he's undermined by a threatened senior player.

- *Flash but No Substance.*   This player impresses upper-level management while alienating everyone else. Pompous, smart, and self-serving at every turn, she does fine as long as nobody she's aggravated on the way up gets ahead faster than she does. This player not only has a keen sense of when to jump ship, but has some mystical quality that makes her eminently hirable. Sometimes lands very senior positions.

- *The Nervous-Nellie Workaholic.*   This player is so insecure about himself and the job he does that he overworks, produces voluminous amounts of material, yet curiously, often comes up short in crucial situations. A good candidate for burnout, this player is taken advantage of by others who get him to do their work. Recognized for what he is by senior management, if he's able to hang in, he becomes a fixture at one spot until retirement.

- *The Attractive Charmer.* Good-looking, widely admired, and socially interactive, this player has to play her cards close to the vest so she doesn't stir up jealousies and get sabotaged by the envious or the rejected. A terrific lunch or let's-work-late partner.

To make matters more difficult for these midlevel corporate players, the cost of money today and the dramatic increase in new product failures, plus the increasingly competitive global markets, have caused many top managements to take away whatever real responsibility they once had. All important decisions are made at the top and delegated down to the middle managers whose job it is to pass the ideas along for execution by junior-level players. If the junior players execute successfully and keep their noses clean—that is, block the flow of any problematic information—then they will eventually move up. Here's an example of the way it works:

A top senior manager tells his team of middle managers to find ways to cut costs on the production of a particular brand of shampoo without affecting customer satisfaction. The middle managers tell the junior players to come up with ideas that will achieve this goal. The junior players do a great deal of research and come up with a number of ideas, all of which contain various pitfalls. The information regarding these potential problems is suppressed because it has been made clear to them that only positive "can do" information is pertinent. The middle managers pass the ideas back to their senior manager. Top management decides on one cost-cutting measure: The shampoo in question contains an expensive, well-known name-brand fragrance, which they will replace with a new, cheaper formula, which negatively affects the lathering of the product, but whose scent lasts longer in the hair. There exists considerable information that suggests that what matters most to consumers is the longevity of the fragrance. Contradictory information, including some that indicates consumers' choice of the product is based on the deep-cleaning lathering process, is suppressed. The middle managers pass the decision along to junior players for execution. If the "new and improved" reformulation is successful, a slight cost increase will be implemented, and the bottom line will have gotten a boost from both ends—production and profit-per-unit. Those involved in making this happen smoothly can look forward to some form of reward. If a problem or problems arise, blame will be distributed in some unpredictable fashion, according to the particular politics of the situation and the general lines of power and entrenchment.

It sounds a bit dismal. And it can be. But there are dozens of counterexamples, times when instead of lowering their standards to meet or beat the competition, a company was somehow forced to do its best to provide the highest quality it could. I was once involved in a story with a positive outcome, for the company and consumers alike. I don't want to blow my own horn, but the story does contain lessons about the real effect of corporate shells.

Years ago I worked for a manufacturer of luxury goods. Early on I discovered that customers were having a lot of trouble with a number of our products. One particular high-ticket product was being returned in alarming numbers, cracked or in pieces. The returns were accompanied by angry letters detailing how the product had broken in the course of common everyday use.

Managers of this manufacturer were preconditioned by top management to refuse to offer replacement in almost all cases and to never give refunds. The corporate shell we hid inside consisted of a letter written to the disappointed customer in which it was implied that the customer was at fault . . . they had mishandled the product resulting in damage . . . the product had been tested under normal conditions . . . no one else had this problem . . . we were sorry but . . .

This policy was contrary to my entire philosophy of doing business—a philosophy that revolved around the idea of making whatever effort was necessary to satisfy the customer. I was convinced that our combative, defensive reaction to customer problems was costing us untold profits. Yet, even as our sales were slumping and our market share declining, the managers fought to preserve our shell. They argued that if we admitted to the possible existence of a problem, the roof would cave in with returns. I insisted that the out-of-pocket costs to us for replacement or refund would not be significant, and we would be more than compensated down the line on account of customer loyalty.

My position in the company was shaky. The infighting was bitter. In meeting after meeting after meeting, managers suggested we adopt various cost-cutting measures, or beef up our advertising, or get involved in some crazy, high-profile public relations stunt. I was a lone wolf, and the only reason I didn't get canned for being a controversial troublemaker was because no moves were being made.

So I would listen in disbelief as different managers described dumbfounding scenarios in which our customers were portrayed as idiots whose greatest talent was finding new ways to destroy our faultless products. When I inquired whether customers had been warned that certain conditions were dangerous to our products, these same managers would turn around and insist that anybody with common sense would know better. It would have been funny if the stakes—including whether I kept my job—hadn't been so high.

I battled on, and finally, out of pure desperation, the company agreed to see what would happen if we instituted my ideas. We offered replacements or refunds to anyone at their request, and we dropped an educational note outlining the conditions unfavorable to certain products. I held my breath.

Fortunately our resurgence was rapid. Our retailers had an easier time selling because they were now confident that the manufacturer stood behind the product. Before long we turned the positive attitude into a marketing tool; then, business really took off. And because we had nothing to hide, the work climate improved also. Everybody was happier.

Unfortunately, the majority of companies still have as much to hide as ever before. The tough decisions that would have to be made to meet their responsibilities fairly are not being made. Their reputation for shoddiness and inefficiency continue to be well deserved. It is these companies with their corporate shells that give consumers so much trouble. Now the time has come to learn how to motivate the players inside these shells, to force them to give you what you deserve.

■ ■ ■

A husband and wife get up in the morning. They make use of a variety of products as they ready themselves for a day at the office. A number of those products do not perform the way they are supposed to: There is a problem with their television cable that makes the picture annoyingly fuzzy; the home workout machine has glitches that make it difficult to manipulate properly; their cordless phone rings twice, then goes dead. As consumers, this husband and wife are intensely frustrated. Frequently that frustration is the subject of some portion of their morning chitchat.

They go off to work. The husband is a public relations executive with a major chemical company. He spends his day trying to quash and minimize the bad press concerning one of their products, which might be causing disease in laboratory animals. The wife is a marketing executive with a major consumer products company. She is working on the release of a new skin product, which is being sold as a protectant against air pollution. She is aware that there is zero scientific evidence to suggest that air pollution is in any way damaging to the skin. But she hopes that the fear of pollution in general will inspire women to seek protection and use this product anyway.

This husband and wife happen to be very decent people. Yet as soon as they enter their offices they undergo a transformation. They no longer think of themselves as consumers (or citizens). Suddenly they are executives and their single-minded purpose is to contribute, however indirectly, to their company's bottom line. The consuming public, of which they are two intensely frustrated members, is now seen as a kind of enemy, a target that must be manipulated and persuaded as necessary. The insulated, adversarial nature of their corporations enables them to do to others exactly what they hate when it is done to them.

Like all executives, they would do well to remember that, in fact, they are consumers (and citizens) first and last.

■ ■ ■

4

■

As Universal as E=MC²: Facts=Power

■

STATEMENT OF PHILOSOPHY

In dealing with companies—from the largest multinationals to local merchants—there is one basic and essential equation: facts = power. If you know how to play your facts right, you'll nearly always get what you're entitled to from companies.

We've already set the scene: You're fed up with inadequate products and services; you've seen your brick walls for what they are and you're not going to be stopped by them anymore; you're aware that combative companies have shells because they're insecure and afraid. Now let's get down to business.

So what do you actually do? What do you need to proceed? What's your leverage? What do you, a single, solitary consumer, have at your disposal against big bad companies with all their tactics?

The answer to each and every one of these questions is the same: FACTS, FACTS, FACTS.

Facts are the cornerstone of your attack. Knowing how to use your facts is all the leverage you'll need to resolve the vast majority of problems in your favor.

THE POWER OF FACTS

There are a lot of reasons why facts pack such a huge wallop.

1. *Facts are neutral.*

Employees of companies are used to being assaulted by consumers—angry, threatening, whining, confused, demanding, chiseling consumers. Facts, however, are drained of emotion. They don't come with any baggage; they simply are what they are, and as such, don't arouse defensiveness or hostility.

2. *Facts are very easy to communicate.*

When trying to tackle a problem, most consumers are somewhat self-conscious. They worry about how they look or sound, how they're coming off. This tends to make them confused, self-contradictory, long-winded, and aggressive. Because facts are the simplest, most direct, most concrete type of communication, they take the pressure of self-presentation off.

3. *Facts tell people you know what you're doing and are serious about asserting your rights.*

Employees of companies (especially executives) have many negative attitudes toward consumers—for example, that they're stupid, helpless, or indifferent. This allows them to think they can brush consumers aside. But if they sense you're well prepared, that, in effect, you're a worthy opponent, they often treat you differently.

4. *Facts enable you to be brief and concise and, therefore, effective.*

We all know people who can stretch a simple story to interminable length by filling it with endless details. But the type of facts you'll learn to use in pursuing resolve from companies are of the bare-bones variety. Stripped down to its essential facts, a problem carries maximum weight. Executives who tune out fluff can't help but be appreciative and more likely responsive. Executives respond to executive summaries. Your story, in effect, should mimic what they are already accustomed to.

5. *Facts create empathy.*

Because facts take the pressure off everybody involved by relieving the situation, as much as possible, of its highly charged emotional and subjective elements, the company employee can concentrate entirely on your problem. The "Us vs. Them" quality of the dynamic is minimized, and the encounter, in whatever form, becomes a matter of two human beings trying to work out a familiar, and quite probably shared, experience.

HOW DO YOU KNOW WHICH FACTS ARE IMPORTANT?

This may seem obvious and logical, but it's surprising how frequently consumers lose sight of which facts will sell their case easily and quickly, as opposed to those facts which simply complicate and cloud the issue.

Here the rule of thumb is: Relevant facts are those the company truly needs to know. For example, say you have a problem with an appliance. The color of the appliance would not be a relevant fact, unless the color coating itself happens to be peeling off. Ask yourself: Does the fact tell the person you're dealing with anything that bears directly on your problem? Does the fact relate to the resolve you are seeking? What, where, when, and who are usually perfectly relevant.

You must decide which facts are the most important. Why? Because you don't want to lose the full attention of your listener or reader. You want them to recognize immediately and exactly what product or service you're talking about, what your problem with that product or service is, what your desired solution is, and then, whether they have the authority to resolve the problem. Be brief, concise, and clear. Use only those facts that are neutral, objective, and nonjudgmental. This will maximize your chance of success.

Here is a relatively simple example. On Monday the eighth you decide to send flowers to your aunt. It is her sixtieth birthday. You specify to the florist that delivery be made on Wednesday the tenth. To guarantee this you pay a fifteen-dollar premium. Two weeks later you receive a card thanking you for your "belated" gift. She tells you Uncle H's birthday is on the twelfth, not hers. She also says she loved the flowers and that they lasted longer than they usually do.

What are the relevant facts? Often it is easier to weed out the irrelevant ones first. Is it relevant when you reached the decision to send flowers? No. Is it relevant that it is your aunt's sixtieth birthday? No. Is it relevant that you received a card? Or that Uncle H's birthday is on the twelfth—which is obviously when the flowers actually arrived. No. Or what she thought of the flowers, or how long they lasted? No and no.

All that is relevant is the fact that you specified a delivery date—the tenth—paid a fifteen dollar premium as a guarantee, and yet the flowers arrived on the twelfth. Three separate facts that bear directly and objectively on the issue.

Now take a more complicated situation. You get a supersaver fare from New York to Chicago that costs x dollars. You pay by personal check. The plane is full. You are seated toward the rear of the plane in seat 32A. The meal they serve en route is bland to your taste. As the plane descends into O'Hare at about 5:30 P.M., you experience tremendous pain in your ears. It feels as if the plane's internal air compression has changed radically. You ask the steward for assistance, but he makes what you take to be a dismissive gesture and mouths, "I'm busy." When you get home your hearing remains partially blocked. Your personal physician tells you your injury is minor, and concurs that the cause of the problem is likely due to improper conditions on the plane. The visit to the doctor costs $75.

So which facts are relevant? Is it relevant that you got a supersaver fare? No. That you paid x dollars and did so by check? No. Does it matter that the plane was full or that you thought the food bland? No.

What are the relevant facts then? Some of them were not included in the story, such as the name of the airline, the flight number, and the date of the flight. What you were told that matters is: the departure and destination cities; the number of your seat (it's possible the air-conditioners malfunctioned in one area and not another); the approximate time of the incident; the cost of your visit to the doctor; and the doctor's agreement as to the probable cause of your trouble.

There were two facts of a somewhat subjective nature that might be brought to bear on the case: that when you asked for help, the attendant motioned at you and mouthed the words, "I'm busy." The rules of thumb to follow here are: Include facts like these *Only When Asked;* when you are asked, *Be Specific.* Don't say, "He made a rude gesture," or "He was hostile." Don't say, "He had an obvious attitude problem," or "He couldn't be bothered with me." These are purely subjective characterizations. Saying, "He made a motion with his hand and seemed to mouth, 'I'm busy,'" is not only more compelling, it prevents your listener from being defensive. So, remember, as far as these types of facts are concerned, *Only When Asked,* and *Be Specific.*

Having a working handle on the relevant facts is key. In the previously described case, for example, if you didn't know the name of the airline, you couldn't even begin to proceed. Or if the customer service representative asked, "What date and flight number was that, please?" and you responded, "Gee, I don't know," how could the person help you even if they wanted to?

Or imagine you have a problem with your coffee maker. You call the manufacturer's 800 number and get an operator who is trained to put you off if he can. "What model is your machine?" he asks. "And when did you make the purchase and from what outlet?" You reply, "I don't know; I think it was a local appliance store, but I can't remember. I bought it some time last year." The operator won't even begin to take you seriously. He'll flick you aside like a slow insect.

So, *Collect Your Facts.*

THE PORTNOY FACT FORM

Collecting your facts is made super easy by the Fact Form. (There is a sample on the next two pages.) (For the purposes of this book, the fact form is typeset for clarity and legibility. When you fill it out yourself writing out the information in handwritten form is obviously the most convenient way to collect the facts, as long as you can reread your own handwriting.) The form shows you step-by-step how to proceed with fact collection. A good idea would be to re-create the form on a separate blank sheet of paper, then make twenty to fifty copies of your own for future use.

PORTNOY'S FACT FORM (SIDE ONE)

<u>Step 1. Product or Service Information</u>

<u>Step 2. Problem Statement</u>

<u>Step 3. Desired Solution</u>
(Proceed to side two, Step 4)

<u>Step 5. Actual Solution/Confirmation Communication–Date</u>

PORTNOY'S FACT FORM (SIDE TWO)

Step 4. Name/Contact   Title/Company   Comments/Action/Date
(Upon completion, proceed to side one, Step 5)

The form is self-explanatory. First, identify the product or service in question. A product identification might be: Black and Decker toaster oven; Model A432; serial number 154326789Q; purchased at Joe's Appliances; located in Elmsford, Ohio; date of purchase, 6/2/89; salesman's name, Pete. A service identification might read: UPS overnight delivery package; mailed from Montclair, New Jersey, to Rockland, Illinois; date of mailing, 3/5/89; cost of mailing, $15.95; handled by Joe.

The next step is to summarize in as few words as possible the nature of your problem. The statement might read: Thermostat settings on the oven do not correspond to actual cooking temperatures. Or: Package mailed 3/5/89 did not arrive until 7/5/89. Try to be as brief and concise as you can, but do not feel restricted. If your problem involves a large number of relevant facts, by all means write them down. For example, if an answering service caused you to miss a number of important business calls, write down each one that is verifiable.

The third step is to state your desired solution. Do you want a refund? (If so, specify what amount.) Or are you interested in product replacement, product repair, reimbursement for expenses incurred (specify the amount), credit (specify), or a letter of apology?

After you've filled out the Fact Form a few times, it's a breeze. However, there's nothing like a little practice. Imagine a product or service problem you've encountered recently and see what you can do. (It's been my experience that after their third or fourth case, filling out and using the Fact Form becomes almost second nature to most people.)

FACT ACCUMULATION

Look on the Fact Form, side two, where it says, Name/Contact. The beauty and power of accumulating facts in this manner is that every contact you make becomes an additional fact in your favor. Each fact adds to your power base. Thus, instead of getting discouraged as you get bounced around inside the blubbery middle of a corporation, you're aware that your story is gaining strength, gathering momentum. Each bit of added leverage renews your sense of purpose and resolve. Because you can say exactly who you talked to and, if necessary, what they said, it's rare you'll get too much of a runaround. Stating your case briefly and concisely, along with the accumulating contacts, shows that you are persistent, makes people take you seriously, and even makes them too wary to just brush you aside.

Think about the difference. You call the telephone company to question your last month's bill because you're sure you've been overcharged. The operator at the billing office agrees, finally, with your assessment. You don't get his/her name. Then your next bill arrives without indicating credit. You're back to square one. This time you get a less accommodating operator. You feel your blood pressure rise.

In the other scenario, you completely fill out your Fact Form. You included the name of the operator and the date of your agreement. This time you call back and are able to specifically ask for someone you have already dealt with successfully. If they happen not to be available, you can tell your new operator that you already spoke to so-and-so on such-and-such a date and that they approved a credit which for some reason was not reflected on your latest bill. Think the new operator will give you any trouble? I doubt it.

The Fact Form is like a great friend who helps you adhere to the real, the solid, the true, the direct, and the good-for-you.

Simply documenting things in this fashion can be stimulating and certainly makes you feel empowered. There are three basic and primary experiences in which your facts and your Fact Form come into play. They are: face-to-face encounters, telephone conversations, and letter writing. Well-documented facts are also essential if you have to use the government, the media, outside agencies, consumer groups, etc. But, in general, if you play your facts right, you'll get the revenge you're entitled to before you have to resort to them.

5.
Face-to-Face

Many consumers dread the thought of trying to resolve a problem by going face-to-face. Fearing the worst, they avoid it whenever possible. Others go in expecting trouble and, sure enough, find it. They have a wretched experience that persists miserably in the mind. But if you know what you're doing, the emotional and psychological difficulties of going face-to-face are alleviated. Under these circumstances, face-to-face becomes an encounter that offers the fastest, easiest, and most effective opportunity for achieving a positive resolve.

• Barbara S. purchased a television cart from a nearby home furnishings store. The item required home assembly. In the course of assembling it, Barbara discovered that two key bolts were missing, rendering the cart unusable. She returned to the store without the cart, intent on getting the necessary bolts. Not remembering which salesclerk handled her transaction, she requested assistance from the first available salesperson. After two encounters that went nowhere, the third clerk informed her that they had never seen her problem before, so it was likely she had misplaced the bolts herself. Incensed, Barbara began yelling, then stormed out vowing never to return. True to her vow, she improvised by using bolts that didn't quite fit. The cart was serviceable but shaky.

• Nancy G. bought a men's wallet as a gift at a famous luxury men's store. When she got home, she changed her mind about the wallet and returned to the store to bring it back. The salesclerk told her she could have a store credit but no cash refund. Since she'd paid in cash, she wanted her money back and insisted on seeing the manager. The manager was out, so she was told she could wait. After what seemed like an eternity, she caved in and reluctantly accepted the credit. The credit was never used.

• Chris A. purchased a watch at a well-known department store. Upon opening the box at home he saw that there was a scratch on the back side of the watch casing. The very next day he returned to the store to exchange it for an unblemished one. His salesclerk passed him along to the manager. The manager examined the watch and insisted it looked fine. A sad comedy ensued in which the two men looking at the same thing disagreed with increasing vehemence about what they saw. Finally, frustrated beyond belief, and feeling hopelessly ineffectual, Chris blew his stack. One fuse lit another and the two men exchanged choice expletives. Before engaging in fisticuffs, Chris withdrew, his head teeming with homicidal thoughts. He felt frustrated, angry, and ripped off.

• In a flush of excited perfectionism, Jane P. rushed out and bought a set of eight crystal wineglasses for use that night at a dinner party she was throwing. Proud of her effort, she was doubly infuriated when she realized that three of the glasses were cracked. The experience tainted the party for her and caused her to fume throughout the night. The following morning she rushed back to the store, descended on her salesclerk, and let loose a pent-up fury about the lousy quality of the store's merchandise, its unforgivable unreliability, etc. The manager hustled over and said if she didn't leave the store immediately, the police would be summoned. Afraid and humiliated on account of having created such a scene, she fled the store and, once outside, burst into tears.

• Peter W., an executive traveling on a tight schedule, was forced to deplane before takeoff because of overboarding. Passengers were informed that the ticket agent would rebook them on the earliest available flight. Feeling tremendous pressure, Peter stormed over to the ticket agent and demanded that his "crisis" receive absolute priority. The ticket agent became defensive, then grew sarcastic. Peter didn't know what to do. Feeling betrayed and helpless, it took him quite a while to get it together enough to call ahead and explain his situation. Forever afterward, he attributed the failure of his eventual meeting to the "unbelievably barbaric treatment" the airline forced him to submit to.

Each of these stories are examples of a face-to-face experience that went very badly. All too typical, they occur many thousands of times a day in our marketplace. For the consumers involved there are three negative aspects to the experiences: 1) The experience engenders terrible feelings—anger, rage, frustration, humiliation and betrayal, to name a few; 2) the consumers don't get the resolve they want and are entitled to; 3) the terrible feelings linger on.

Following the guidelines set forth in this chapter will enable you to do away with problems one and three. You simply won't have to worry anymore about having an unpleasant experience.

Where once there was confrontation, now there will be easygoing encounters. What a relief.

As for problem two, you will maximize the possibility of obtaining whatever resolve—refund, replacement, repair, or credit—you decide upon. My own success ratio in these circumstances is 90 percent plus. Let's see how it's done.

WHEN TO USE FACE-TO-FACE

The face-to-face method is the best initial approach when dealing with:

- *Portable Products*
    - Personal Items (cosmetics, jewelry, clothing, etc.)
    - Small Appliances (toasters, blenders, small TV's, radios, etc.)
- *Product Service Repair*
- *Automotive Repair*
- *Ticket Reissue or Refund*
- *Accidental Occurrences*

Because face-to-face is such an excellent method, use it whenever possible. In other words, if I can physically return the product, I do it. This means that if you've received merchandise through the mail or had it delivered, make the return in person.

Services and other problems are better dealt with over the phone—at least initially. (See the following chapter for explanation.)

THE DRAWBACKS AND PITFALLS OF FACE-TO-FACE

We live in a time when decorum and courtesy are not exactly at a premium. This is very much reflected in the manners and attitudes of the people who staff many retail concerns. Such people are frequently beleaguered, rude, hostile, or indifferent. Also, they tend to be neither well trained nor motivated. Never be surprised by ugly behavior. Here are four of the most common and difficult personalities one is likely to be confronted by.

THE INTIMIDATOR.   This clerk/manager lives for the opportunity to make customers squirm. Acutely aware and resentful of the higher economic status of their clientele, he seizes every opportunity to make you feel diminished, incompetent, and frustrated. Specifically, what he does to try to make you feel lousy is irrelevant. What you have to keep in mind is that your reaction—anger, frustration—is his victory. No matter what he does, don't rise to his bait. Keeping your composure causes the edge he normally thrives on to evaporate.

THE TABLE TURNER.   This employee either says it outright or implies that your problem is "your problem." Faulty merchandise is "your fault." Evasive to begin with, she becomes even more so if pressed. Because she identifies with what she is selling, she takes any problem you might have personally. Again, don't rise to her bait. Getting her to switch allegiance and to identify with you is easy if you tread lightly but firmly.

THE BRUSHER-OFFER.   This employee would try to avoid getting involved if your shoes were to suddenly burst into flames. His tune goes: "I can't help you . . . I don't have any idea who can . . . Why don't you come back some other time?" Sometimes entire stores have this atmosphere; no one seems to admit to the slightest degree of authority. Again, be cool. Employees like these tend to sharpen up as soon as polite questions about the store's ownership are asked. Their lackadaisical, discouraging manner does not stand up to the possibility of official reprimand or humiliation.

THE DISPLACED LAWYER.   This clerk/manager acts as if she is on the opposite side in a court of law. She appears to be willing to say anything to punch holes in your story. It's as if she's exercising her wasted intellect looking for some ridiculous loophole on the basis of which she can deny your request. Again, do not rise to her bait. Arguing the finer points will lead nowhere. Like the Brusher-Offers, these types tend to quiver at the mention of higher authority.

These are surely among the most infuriating personalities one is apt to encounter. There is one main key to handling these and all other personalities: *Do not rise to their bait; do not react.* It doesn't matter who they are, what they say, or what they do. Personality is *not* the issue; personality is completely beside the point. Since you can't control the moods, attitudes, or personalities of others, don't try to. If they need to compete with you—ridicule, snub, ignore, or outmaneuver you—fine, let them be them. That's their right. Remember: What goes around comes around.

YOUR ACTION STRATEGY

Transactions are a two-way street. Inasmuch as many store employees don't display ideal human qualities, neither do many of the customers they are used to serving. Employees are regularly assailed by consumers who seem to believe that obnoxious, rude, pushy, and aggressive behavior is both appropriate and necessary. Interviews with store employees reveal that there is one, altogether too common, type of consumer that they have to be on guard against. This customer arrives at the store primed for battle. They are determined to beat any and all store personnel into total submission. They don't want assistance—their aim is to vanquish, humiliate, and get someone fired.

Girded to withstand or deflect such attackers, some employees adopt a difficult, but skin-deep, demeanor as an act of self-preservation. So be apprised: You may have to initially pay for the Neanderthal behavior of a few others.

How then should you behave? There are a few key guidelines. In the first place, do not make the mistake of confusing aggression with assertion. Aggression is negative; assertion is positive. Aggression breeds aggression or defensiveness and anger; assertion indicates that you have rights and are pursuing them. Aggression forces you and the interaction to become the focus; assertion keeps it squarely on the issue where it belongs.

Keep in mind the old adage: Treat others as you would like them to treat you. And don't be superficial about it; don't expect anything in return. Be persistently decent and polite. If you can't say something nice, don't say anything at all. Acting well, being a good person, not only makes you feel good about yourself, it eventually disarms even some of the biggest ax grinders.

And, finally, drain yourself—and the situation—of as much emotion as you can. This is not an occasion for psychological, emotional, or interpersonal complexity.

Yes, the inherent reality of the face-to-face encounter is highly charged. Yes, under ordinary circumstances human beings affect each other enormously and have enormous trouble with each other. But this is not an ordinary circumstance. It is a contrived situation wherein you have a specific goal. Achieving that goal is up to you. If you allow the experience to feel like a confrontation, things are likely to go badly. But if you remain objective and unemotional, regardless of the provocation, the outcome is usually positive.

Remember: You are in the driver's seat, as cool, calm, collected, and unflappable as a race car driver. You are not guaranteed to win the encounter, it may not lead to the resolve you're seeking (though it usually does), but at least you won't feel awful either during or afterward.

HOW TO HANDLE FACE-TO-FACE ENCOUNTERS

First: Prepare your facts using the Fact Form. Always use the Fact Form. It will force you to get your thoughts in line, be certain of the ground you stand on, and be reminded of the solution you are seeking and deserve. If you can, memorize the facts. If not, use the form as a crib sheet. Whatever you do in this regard, you will appear organized and prepared.

Second: If possible, return the product to the retail concern in its original packaging, accompanied by the original receipt. The receipt usually identifies the salesperson, the amount paid, the form of payment (all of which you should recite from your Fact Form), and most importantly, proves you purchased the item from that particular store. It is a good idea to make a copy of the sales receipt before returning to the store because sometimes it disappears in the course of your pursuit. If you've thrown the receipt away or lost it, try to remember the pertinent information as best you can. How you act and what you say are the real determinants.

Third: If possible, arrive at the store at an hour when it is less likely to be crowded. Lunchtime and closing time are bad times. Middle of the morning or afternoon are good times.

Fourth: Ask specifically for the salesperson from whom you purchased the item in question. If he or she is not available, immediately ask for the department manager or store manager.

THE BASIC STRUCTURE OF A FACE-TO-FACE ENCOUNTER

Ready yourself mentally. If you've had a bad day or are in a bad mood, leave. Otherwise, drain yourself of emotion. Remind yourself to stay on an even keel no matter what happens. Remind yourself that you are on a mission, a mission that you're in complete control of and that you're actually looking forward to.

Approach the appropriate salesclerk or manager. Stand straight and look him in the eye. Smile. Nod. Begin the encounter with pleasantries. Say something complimentary about the store and/or merchandise you've purchased there. Ask how he is, how his day is going.

Next: Say you are a loyal customer with a small problem. Deliver your problem statement. Be brief, concise, and clear.

Next: State your desired solution (refund, replacement, repair, credit).

Next: If the clerk/manager responds with any obstacle, ask: What's your opinion? What would you do if you were me? Repeat your problem statement: I bought it here on such-and-such a date, then . . .

Next: If no assistance is forthcoming at this point, politely ask: Do you have the authority to help me? Then say: I really don't want you to get in trouble by exceeding your authority. If he says no, or worse, ask: Could you please direct me to someone who might help me with my problem? Get the name and title.

Next: Tell him you appreciate his help and wish him a good day. (It's surprising how often an employee will change his mind and offer assistance at this, the last second.)

Proceed to the suggested party. Do precisely as before, except before giving your problem statement, give the name of the person who sent you and say: I understand that so-and-so is not empowered to resolve my problem, but I'm told that you're the person I should talk to. (Telling people that they have the authority sometimes causes them to act as if they do).

Next: Follow the same format.

Next: If they put you off in any way, politely request the name of the store owner or corporate manager. Say: I realize you're in a difficult position. Under the circumstances you've been very helpful. Perhaps the best way for me to get resolve is with the owner or manager of the store. What are the names and how might I reach them?

This tends to have a very motivating effect on many employees.

Next: Write down the contacts you've already made on your Fact Form. Briefly and objectively spell out what has been said to you thus far. Remember: When you reach the right person, *Be Specific* and use the comments *Only When Asked.*

If you reach this juncture without getting what you want, it's time to proceed to the next method—the telephone. It has been my experience that store owners or corporate level managers of retail concerns not only don't know anything about any employees other than the manager, but are aghast when contacted, and will bend over backward to make things right if you've got your facts in order and know what you're doing.

THE WAY IT SHOULD WORK (AND USUALLY DOES)

I purchased several ties and shirts from a small men's store on New York's West Side. Once at home I realized that two of the ties did not really match the suits I had intended to wear them with. So I decided to return them. Using my Fact Form, I set out the following: Two ties, costing x amount; the problem statement said that the ties did not match the suits for which I'd bought them; the desired solution was a refund.

I returned to the store with my original receipt and packaging. I greeted my salesman warmly and told him how happy I was with my new shirts. Then I delivered my problem statement and desired solution. To my surprise, he told me the store had a credit-only policy. I told him I didn't know this and didn't see it posted in the store. He insisted: It's store policy; no refund. I told him I sympathized with his position and asked to see the manager.

I repeated my story to the manager, adding that I didn't know the store's policy or see it posted anywhere. He concurred that there was no sign, but nevertheless balked. I asked him how he would handle the situation if he were me? After a moment's reflection, he agreed a refund was in order. He said he would put up a notice stating the store's return policy and thanked me. We parted on excellent terms and I have received kid-glove treatment at the store ever since.

A PARTING CAUTIONARY NOTE

Don't expect things to go without a hitch your first or even second time out. Like anything else, it takes a little practice before you get the knack. And when you do, feel free to develop your own style, to be a bit creative. As long as you stick to the main guidelines, though, face-to-face encounters will reward you with a high rate of success.

▪ ▪ ▪

Anytime you plan to make a purchase in a retail concern, always check to see what the store's return policy is. In most states, by law they can't invoke a policy unless they post it. If you don't see it anywhere, ask: Is your return policy posted? If not, ask: What is your return policy?

There are many ways to get leverage before you engage in a purchase. As a general rule, get the name of anybody you deal with and make a note of it. Then, do not throw away the packaging your purchase comes in until you're sure it's a keeper (at least for the time being). Also, it's a very good idea to keep a receipt file. In fact, keeping receipts is a critical way of strengthening your case; it's not the end of the world if you don't have your receipts, but if you have them they will facilitate the fact collection process as well as documentation procedures. Finally, if you don't see the name and address of the manufacturer, ask for it before you run into problems. People tend to be more helpful before you've paid than after.

A word to the wise: If you have a problem with a particular store, avoid it unless you get quick, easy resolve. Patronize stores that make customer service a priority.

▪ ▪ ▪

6

·

The Phone as a Consumer Weapon

■

STATEMENT OF PHILOSOPHY

Most people use the telephone a great deal. They consider themselves adept if not masterful at it. However, using the phone to get what you deserve from a company is a special matter, separate and distinct from the electronic interactions one is familiar with. What you should say and what you have to listen for are not the same as in ordinary, normal conversation.

• Alan N. bought a major-brand microwave from a no-frills discount retailer. Within weeks, the microwave couldn't melt an ice cube. When the retailer refused to service or replace the unit, Alan called the manufacturer. Being an affable fellow, he got passed from person to person and had a number of lively, pleasant conversations—each of which ended without there being a hint of resolve. Eventually, he wound up talking to a Colin G., who abruptly suggested he purchase himself a new unit from a reputable dealer, and then hung up. Discouraged, Alan did just that.

• Jane D. called a major electronics company 800 hot-line number to find out why her new big-screen television, which was hooked up to a cable TV connection, wasn't delivering as good a picture as her old set. The recorded message told her to press the number two on her touch-tone phone if she wanted technical assistance. After an automated voice said, "You are now being connected with the party you requested," there was a period of silence. Then another automated voice came on and informed her, "All our technicians are busy. Please call back later." Jane did this a half dozen times with the same results, then gave up, unhooked the wire, and settled for much less than perfect reception.

• Lisa S. received a notice from her bank indicating she was overdrawn on her account. She knew this wasn't possible; yet because she wrote a lot of checks, she was concerned that if a lot of bouncing occurred, her credit rating would suffer. She called her bank and was told by the woman who answered that she should call a different branch. The man who now answered told her the person who handled overdraws was on another line and would call her back. When no call came, Lisa called back. The same man said the same thing and Lisa lost her temper. "I happen to be an important customer, and you better get off your butt, buddy. Why don't you just check the computer and see what the problem is with my account." The man replied, "Because I don't have to." Then he hung up.

The telephone can be a very potent instrument for resolving bad consumer experiences. If you know who to call and what to say, using the phone to get what you're entitled to can be as automatic as picking it up to shoot the breeze. As one friend of mine put it, "If I have a problem with something I've paid for, I'd just as readily handle it by phone as order Chinese takeout."

To be sure, the phone has a number of natural advantages when compared to face-to-face encounters. 1) You don't have to travel. 2) You, in effect, have the whole world at your fingertips; if it takes a dozen contacts in different locations to get what you're after, fine. 3) You don't have to worry about being badly abused or worry about getting into a terrible fight—the phone is simply not as emotionally charged or as potentially volatile. Provocations over the phone don't have the same sting. 4) You're not as self-conscious. You don't have the awful worry about being judged on the basis of your looks, clothes, physical stature, age, or body language; the phone is a great equalizer. 5) You can take notes on what transpires. 6) You can go back to the same person again and again, armed with new facts, without getting tired out.

On the other hand, because most people are relaxed and confident on the phone, they have a greater tendency to make certain fatal mistakes. 1) They become chatty, beat around the bush, act like what they're looking for is an enjoyable interaction. 2) Because they're invisible, some people take the opportunity to role-play. They try to come off as a celebrity, a power broker, a big shot, a tough banana. Any attempt to show off smudges the focus and is counterproductive. 3) Because the other person can't be seen, they too easily take for granted that whatever he says, he's just doing his job. Never be a sucker for a nice, polite dismissal; being blown away is being blown away.

WHEN TO USE THE PHONE

If, for whatever reason—distance, inconvenience, illness, disinclination—you are unable to return to the point of purchase, use the phone.

If you've failed to get satisfaction through your face-to-face encounters, use the phone.

If you've written a letter(s) and not gotten satisfactory response, use the phone.

The phone is the tool of first resort if you have a problem with any of the following:

- *Nonportable Products*
    - Major Household Appliances
    - Furniture
    - Heavy Equipment
- *Services*
    - At Home Repairs
    - Billing Problems, Hotels, Car Rentals, Utility Companies, etc.
    - Banking/Financial Matters
- *Direct-Mail Purchases*
- *Nontangibles*
    - Insurance

The basic procedure for handling all problems with products and services by phone is the same. You don't have to worry about knowing all the kinds of subtleties and tricks.

WHO TO CALL

In virtually every circumstance, begin trying to resolve your problem by *contacting the person you did business with.*

If your problem is with a small retail concern, ask for the salesperson who handled your transaction. This information will be on your receipt. If that individual is unavailable or unhelpful, ask for the department or store manager. If the store is privately owned, ask for the owner.

If it's a service company, get in contact with the person who served you. If he or she is not available, ask for the service adviser. Then the owner.

In general, if the owner is on-site, you should deal with him or her. And always call the local level first. (The telephone number will be in the phone book or can be obtained through directory assistance.)

If you've exhausted your possibilities at the local level, it's time to move on to the manufacturer or parent company. Always ask for the customer service department. If one doesn't exist, ask for billing/credit or technical staff (repairs).

There are many ways to get the telephone number you want. You can ask a retailer, including the one from whom you've made your purchase, to check the packaging or the carton. If they ask why, say you want to find out if it's American-made. You can get the name of the company from your own packaging, off the product itself, or from your receipt or billing statement. Then call directory assistance in that area.

Some companies list toll-free numbers right on their products. You can also call 800-555-1212 for company hot-line numbers, or buy a directory of toll-free consumer numbers from AT&T (to order, call 800-426-8686).

If there is no local listing for the corporation and no toll-free number, go to your local library and check the *Standard & Poor's Register of Corporations and Directors and Executives.*

If you can't find out who even manufactured the product in question, go to the library and check the *Thomas Register of American Manufacturers* or the *Thomas Register Catalog File.* This reference lists the brand names and makers of most products.

GENERAL BEHAVIOR FOR GIVING GOOD PHONE

1. *Be courteous and polite at all times.* As with face-to-face encounters, don't lose your cool regardless of the provocation. If you rise to their bait with anger or rudeness, you'll be on their hook.

2. *Be unemotional.* Don't get excited or carried away because slipups can occur, plus the purpose of your call can get buried or obscured.

3. *Be assertive when stating your desired solution, but never be aggressive or insistent.* Aggression makes people defensive; assertion indicates seriousness and preparedness.

4. *Always be brief, concise, and to the point.* It saves you time and energy (you may have to repeat your story several times). Also, executives appreciate it and it keeps your problem directly in focus.

5. *Be tenacious.* The phone is different than face-to-face in this regard. With the phone you may have to have a large number of contacts. But just remember: Each one is an addition to your power base; every new contact and what they say should be jotted down on your Fact Form for future reference.

BASIC TELEPHONE TACTICS/PROCEDURE

1. *Fill out your Fact Form.* Familiarize yourself with its contents. Have a pen or pencil at hand for writing down names, titles, and if you like, short notes.

2. *Call the number.* If an automated operator or an operator trained to discourage you answers, use *Standard & Poor's* to get the name and number of an executive in charge of customer service. If none exists, get the head of billing/credit

or technical staff (repairs). If none exists, get the name of the company president and use the president's secretary tactic described on page 70.

3. *Always greet the person who answers warmly.* If he offers his name, say, "Hello ———," then give your name. If he doesn't give his name, ask for it—"Who am I talking to?"—then say, "Hello ———, this is ———." The point is to immediately personalize the call, and repeating the name right away will help you remember it.

4. *Ask to speak to customer service.* If they want to know what your call is in reference to, say, "An issue relating to one of your products." If they still resist, state your facts, problem, and desired solution. They will either help you or pass you along.

5. *If passed along to a customer service representative, repeat your greeting and pertinent information.*

6. *Be a good listener.* It's vital that you listen to his response and evaluate it. Is he eager or willing to assist you?

7. *If not, ask, "Please, Mr. Jones. Do you have the authority to help me resolve my problem?"* This question is pressure point number one.

8. *If he says he can't help you or tries to stall you in any way ("I'll have to check this and get back to you," or "I'm just not sure how to handle this," or "I don't think there's anything anybody here can do for you"), then say, "Mr. Jones, is there anybody else who has the authority to make this decision, possibly your supervisor?"* This shows that you won't be stonewalled and gives him an opportunity to redeem himself. If he balks, ask, "May I please have the name of the person you report to?" Offer your thanks to Mr. Jones to reduce any brewing hostility. Then call back and ask to be directly connected to the higher level of authority. These are pressure points numbers two and three.

9. *If he indicates he does have the authority to assist you,*

say, "Mr. Jones. Please turn your desk around for a moment.
What would you do, how would you handle this problem if you
were me?" There is no more disarming question. It flatters
him, takes him out of his normal mode, and reminds him that
he too is a consumer. This is pressure point number four.

10. *If, on the other hand, he tells you there is someone else*
who might help you, and tells you the person will call you back,
ask for the person's name and title, "so I can expect their
call," then offer polite thanks and hang up. *But don't wait.*
Call-backs often never come. Make the call yourself, asking for
the person by name and title and saying you were referred by
Mr. Jones.

11. *Each time you talk to a new person, greet him by name,*
give him your facts, problem statement, and desired solution;
then tell him with whom you've already spoken. Listen carefully and evaluate his response.

SPECIAL TACTIC: THE PRESIDENT'S SECRETARY

If you receive resistance all the way through the head of customer service, it is often very effective to call the president's
office. (Ask the main operator for the president's secretary;
asking for the president won't always get you connected.)

These secretaries are highly trained and highly competent
individuals. They also want to screen the boss from whatever
problems they can. So, greet them warmly by name; say you
are a loyal customer of the company; state your facts, deliver
your problem statement, state your desired solution, then recap
the action you've taken thus far—contacts and a summary
statement of why the previous contacts couldn't be of assistance. Then ask, repeating the secretary's name, "What do you
think my next step should be?" More often than not, they will

give you a name to call. Sometimes they will call ahead on your behalf.

If they can't help you directly, it's still a wonderful contact; another pressure point. Call back the head of customer service, and say you've been speaking to the president's secretary (by name). This is often more credible and motivating than invoking the president's name.

WHEN THE PRESIDENT'S SECRETARY ISN'T HELPFUL

If the president's secretary stonewalls completely, write a letter to the president (see next chapter). Send it Federal Express (to make sure it gets opened). Say that you've made repeated attempts to reach him by phone. State your problem, desired solution, and say you'd appreciate prompt consideration. Then, call back and indicate you're making a follow-up call to a recently sent letter. Or say, "Mr. X is expecting my call."

If this doesn't work, you'll have to pursue a higher authority (see chapter 17). You might indicate in a second letter to the president that you are about to do this; doing so gives him one last chance to redeem himself.

A VARIATION: PRODUCTS THAT REQUIRE SERVICING AT HOME

Suppose you have a washing machine that either requires servicing or has been serviced many times without being fixed. Here's how to handle the situation:

1. Fill out the Fact Form.
2. Call the retailer from whom you bought the item and

ask for your salesperson. If they're not available, speak only to the manager or owner.

3. Identify the product, problem, and desired solution, which, in this case, is repair or unit replacement. Ask that a service person be sent to fix the item. Get them to tell you who they will be assigning and when they will be arriving.

4. Confirm the appointment by phone the day before with the manager or owner.

5. If the service work is unsatisfactory, or the person doesn't show up, call the manager or owner immediately.

6. They will have an excuse and will want to reschedule. But do not wait.

7. Contact the corporate headquarters for the product. If you're not sure who makes it, check the *Thomas Register*.

8. Call and follow the basic procedure, asking for customer service. Give your story, adding one point: the fact that the retailer from whom you purchased the item is having trouble repairing it, or that the service person isn't showing up. Ask if the manufacturer has their own repair staff or if they have a regional distributor (a wholesaler) who maintains such a staff. The manufacturer's people or distributor will be better equipped to resolve the problem. If repair is difficult, they will more readily authorize replacement. (A local retailer will avoid replacement at all costs.)

9. In some cases the manufacturer or distributor will contact the retailer directly and insist they service the product immediately and satisfactorily. Once the retailer knows you have these people involved, they tend to act vigorously.

10. If you are verbally promised a new unit, confirm it in writing with the manufacturer, the distributor, and the retailer (if they are going to be responsible for delivery).

11. If the problem continues, update your Fact Form, call the director of customer service, and proceed as before.

12. If this doesn't work, use the president's secretary tactic.

13. When the problem has been resolved, send a thank-you note to the person deemed most responsible (see chapter 7).

Here's an example of a successful phone encounter that illustrates these principles.

I purchased a fax machine and had no problems sending communications overseas. But one Italian-based company had trouble faxing me back. There was always a breakdown on the line. I filled out my Fact Form. Contacted the retailer, who proved to be of no help at all. Called 800-555-1212 and got the number of the manufacturer. Their automated operator told me to press two for technician assistance. After three attempts—disconnected twice, once put on eternal hold—I went to *Standard & Poor's,* from which I obtained the name and number of the person in charge of customer service. I followed my procedure to the letter, but got zero satisfaction. Then I called the main operator and asked to be connected to the president's secretary.

I was put through to a Ms. Miller and I told her right away how much I liked my new fax machine. Then I told her my problem and desired solution—repair or replacement. Then I described what had happened to me thus far in trying to get resolve. She was "very concerned" about what had occurred with the automatic operator. She asked to put me on hold briefly, and tried the number herself. Minutes later, she came back on the line and apologized profusely for the trouble. She promised it would be taken care of, then put me in touch with a senior technician, who explained to me over the phone how to make the necessary adjustment on the machine that alleviated the fax reception problem. The phone was an end unto itself. I didn't have to go further than the use of the phone to get the resolve I wanted.

▪ ▪ ▪

New York, New York, is a great, great city. It is also a tough, tough town. Perhaps it's true that if you can make it there, you can make it anywhere; it's certainly true that if you are trying to resolve a consumer problem, especially by phone, try to do it elsewhere. If the company has regional corporate offices in New York, but is headquartered in another part of the country, bypass the regional office, even if you live in New York, and call straight to the headquarters. People who work in New York tend to be more hard-edged, less sympathetic, less likely to take the time to be of assistance. I can't tell you how many times when trying to help a New Yorker with a problem, I've run into a dead end with the representatives in New York, then gotten satisfaction with ease by calling company offices or headquarters somewhere else in the United States.

Another interesting aspect of this phenomenon is that when executives hear that you are calling from New York, they are especially gracious and accommodating. I've been told by business people from other parts of the country that because New York gets so much good and bad attention and exposure, they are inclined to want to impress you, and show you how differently—i.e., more humanely—they do things.

▪ ▪ ▪

7

Simple, Effective Letter Writing

Modern communications technology has caused people to get out of the habit of writing letters. Some people are actually intimidated because they've entirely forgotten how to do it. To this day, however, letters that are short, simple, and to the point have a great impact on executives. In fact, there are circumstances in which a letter—and only a letter—will get you what you want.

• Allie B. bought a "new" facial cream made by one of the big-name cosmetic companies. The product was advertised as nonallergenic, yet upon using it, Allie immediately developed a severe skin problem. The dermatologist who treated her said her problem could not be positively tied to her use of the product, thereby negating the viability of a lawsuit. Nevertheless, convinced that her problem was a reaction to the facial cream, Allie determined to at least get compensated for the cost of her medical bills. She sent a letter to the president of the company in which she furiously blasted them for false advertising, plus threatened all sorts of legal action unless she received full compensation. The letter was never responded to.

• Tanya P. decided to leave her job as a graphic designer and free-lance. To this end she invested a great deal of money in a computer that had the capability of doing sophisticated computer graphics. Two months after making the purchase she began to have trouble with the computer. The retailer serviced it twice, both times to no avail, then refused to offer the replacement unit that was clearly called for. At her wit's end, Tanya wrote a letter to the manufacturer. Her letter read like a long treatment for a screenplay. In elaborate detail she described the emotional backdrop of the various funny-but-not-so-funny business difficulties she had suffered on account of the computer. She addressed her appeal, which ran some nine pages, "To Whom It May Concern." Apparently nobody was particularly concerned: She received a polite reply thanking her for her "interesting story" and wishing her luck in her future endeavors.

• James M. had work done on his apartment by a large, reputable contracting firm. At some point while the work was being done, his very expensive sound system was blown out. Neighbors told him the workmen had continuously played the system at top volume. James got in touch with the owner of the firm by telephone. After speaking with his subcontractors, the owner agreed to provide full restitution for any repairs. However, when a month passed without receiving money as per their verbal agreement, James contacted the owner again. At first the owner claimed not to remember their conversation, then he adamantly denied having made any commitment.

"How am I supposed to know how or when your system got busted?" he said.

• A vacation promotion company in Miami sent thousands of postcards telling recipients that they had been chosen to receive "fabulous luxury cruises at unbelievable discount rates." Vickie W. was thrilled. She called the company number and fell for the telemarketer's ploy: "Give us your credit card number now in order not to lose out later. If you change your mind, all you have to do to cancel is give us a call." She did change her mind, but when she returned the vacation certificates by regular mail, no credit appeared on her next billing statement. Vickie called her credit card company and they told her to send them a letter, along with documentation proving she had returned the certificates. Because she had neglected to return the certificates by registered mail, providing her with a return receipt, the company was unable to help her.

Most people don't write letters of any kind anymore. Not only are they out of the habit of communicating in this manner, they are intimidated at the prospect of having to "write." They imagine that in order to get results, their letters would have to be clever, creative, articulate, and persuasive. This is not the case at all.

Then there are other people who do write letters, but make mistakes that completely undermine their effort. They don't know who to write to or what to say (and what not to say). Whether they take the opportunity to vent their spleen, make extravagant threats and demands, or write a lengthy history of their experience, they make it easy for their would-be respondent to dismiss and ignore them.

The simple fact of the matter is that in order to be effective, a letter must follow very definite rules. Adherence to the rules makes letter writing a wonderful way of achieving the justice you seek from companies. Wonderful, in part, because it's such a snap.

WHEN TO USE LETTER WRITING

To begin with, any problem that has not been resolvable through a face-to-face encounter or by using the telephone should be tackled by letter.

Secondly, don't let what happened to James M. happen to you. *Use letter writing to confirm all verbal agreements!* Sadly, we live at a time when verbal agreements or commitments are often not kept after the fact. Thus, whether you get a commitment in person or over the phone, follow up immediately with a letter confirming your agreement and send it to the individual with whom you had success. Send the letter by registered, certified, or overnight mail, return receipt requested, and keep a copy yourself. This way the recipient can't deny receiving it.

Letter writing is frequently the second or third tool at your disposal in pursuing remedy. However, there are five circumstances in which it is your tool of first resort.

1. *In any transaction in which you paid by credit card, use letter writing to document any action you take.* (Again, use registered, certified, or overnight mail, return receipt requested, and keep a copy.) In order to take advantage of your legal rights via the Fair Credit Billing Act (see pages 93–94), you must document all your action and put your problem in writing within sixty days of billing.

2. *Use letter writing when you have a problem with a high-ticket item (car, house, boat, etc.) or a costly service (expensive hotel visit).* In most cases, where a significant amount of money is at stake, companies are more likely to respond to documentation set in black and white.

3. *If your problem is complex or involves a large number of facts, it's best to put it in writing right away.* It's much easier for someone trying to help you to be able to read your story than it is for her to have to listen to a phone call and take extensive notes.

4. *Use letter writing if you have a recurrent problem or a problem that won't go away.* Supposing your washing machine is serviced five times, but still doesn't work properly. Don't call; the time has come to write the manufacturer and ask them to send their own technical professional to fix or assess the problem. Then, if the unit is not reparable, they can authorize a replacement.

5. *Any communication with the media or any authority resource should be done in writing.* They will usually request that you do so anyway. Also, if you've written any other letters—to a regional distributor or to the manufacturer—include copies. Authorities and the media love written documentation—the more of it you have, the more quickly and supportively they will react.

Optional: Use letter writing to show your appreciation to anyone who has been instrumental in helping you. Everyone appreciates being stroked. A thank-you note will put you in good stead in the event you have another problem with the same company. You can't put a price on goodwill.

WHOM TO WRITE TO

It is vital that your letter be sent to a particular person. You must know the exact name. Writing "Owner, John's Parts," or "Customer Service Director," or "To Whom It May Concern" is no good. If your problem is with a small business, write the owner, by name. In dealings with a large company, write to the person in charge of consumer relations. If you have not had a satisfactory response from the person in charge of consumer problems, write to the president of the company, by name. If your problem is with a product or service distributor, and their consumer relations department has not responded to your letter satisfactorily, write to the regional corporate manager, whose job is to oversee the distributor in question. (Always include a copy of any previous communications.)

Again, it is imperative that the exact name of the individual you are trying to reach be on the envelope and in your salutation. The name of the right person can be obtained by calling the company. Some companies even list toll-free numbers on their products. Remember, you can also call 800-555-1212 for information or buy a directory of toll-free consumer numbers from AT&T (to order, call 800-426-8686).

If there is no local listing for the corporation and no toll-free number, use the *Standard & Poor's Register of Corporations and Directors and Executives,* available at your library. If you have no idea who even manufactured your product, check the *Thomas Register of American Manufacturers* or the *Thomas Register Catalog File,* also available at your library. This reference provides the brand names and makers of thousands of products.

GENERAL GUIDELINES FOR LETTER WRITING

1. Always type letters or get them typed. Handwritten communications are not taken as seriously.

2. Make and keep a copy of all written communications for your file.

3. Keep your letter to one page. Executives handle a huge

flow of paperwork. They appreciate brevity and conciseness, as their own memos and executive summaries attest to. In all cases, shorter is better.

4. Type single-spaced. Executives are used to a certain format; imitating that format is key.

5. If there are a lot of facts pertinent to your story, use bullets (•) to set each one off, line-by-line.

  • I met with Mr. X on March 5th.
  • I phoned Ms. Y on March 10th.

6. Make and include copies of all pertinent documents: sales receipts, warranties, repair or service orders, canceled checks, contracts, etc. (You keep the originals.)

7. If you have a service problem, for example, a caterer who left your house in a shambles, or a maintenance company that damaged a piece of furniture, take a photograph of the problem and include it as further documentation.

8. Always address your letter to a specific person, using their exact name and title.

9. Always send your letter via certified, registered, or overnight mail, return receipt requested. That way no one can claim they never received your letter.

10. Wait a maximum of *three weeks* for a response. If you receive no response in that time period, try to reach the person to whom you have written by telephone. If you get a secretary who is running interference and wants to know the reason for your call, don't launch into your story. That may lead to a deferral ("Ms. Peters is in a meeting," where you can bet she'll be whenever you call for the rest of your life). Tell the secretary that you sent Ms. Peters a letter dated XYZ, and say she is expecting your follow-up call. (If your letter was sent to the president of the company, use the secretary-to-the-president telephone method outlined in the previous chapter.)

11.   If your action up to this point still gets no results, you will have to pursue a higher authority (see chapter 17).

WRITING THE LETTER

Your tone should be firm and clear. As when using any of the tools, do not be emotional or subjective. Resist the temptation to be angry, threatening, demanding, or nasty. You aren't trying to raise a ruckus; you are seeking results. Assertion, in the form of stating your desired solution, is the proper stance. Do not even try to be clever, articulate, or persuasive. The format itself gives you all the weight and force you need.

Now:

1.   Take your Fact Form and minimally flesh out the facts on a sheet of paper. Identify the product; where you purchased it; the date of the purchase; the model or serial number. In the case of a service, identify the service rendered; the person or persons who provided it; the date it was rendered; the cost.

2.   Describe any action you have taken prior to the letter—contacts made and the dates of those contacts; personal visits, phone calls, etc.

3.   State your problem as briefly as possible.

4.   State your desired solution.

5.   Give telephone numbers where you can be reached day and night, and the best times to do so.

6.   Think of an ending you are comfortable with: "Thank you for your cooperation," "I look forward to hearing from you," "I have always admired your company," etc.

Now transfer this information onto a fresh sheet. Your letter should be set up like this:

Date

Name of person
Title
Name of company
Street address
City and state

Re: Here summarize the subject of the letter. This helps the executive know immediately what you are writing about.

Dear Ms. Smith:

Give the facts. (If there are a lot of them, use bullets.)

Deliver your problem statement.

Indicate the action you have taken to date.

State your desired solution.

Say where you can be reached by phone day and night and the best times to do so. Say a nice word and offer thanks.

Sincerely,
Your signature
Your typed name

This is the basic format. As one of the samples that follow shows, it varies slightly if you are writing to confirm an agreement. Now take a look at the samples and, if possible, practice the procedure on your own once or twice.

PORTNOY'S FACT FORM (SIDE ONE)

<u>Step 1. Product or Service Information</u>
Courtesy Rental Car 2/21/89–2/23/89
San Francisco Airport
Taurus station wagon—Contract #104023

<u>Step 2. Problem Statement</u>
Rear tailgate malfunction prevented full use of car.
No other vehicles available at the time.
Problem discovered after picking up car at airport.

<u>Step 3. Desired Solution</u>
(Proceed to side 2, Step 4)
Reduced rate/Refund

<u>Step 5. Actual Solution/Confirmation Communication–Date</u>
Received reduced rate on rental car.
Refund of $34.55.
Sent back-up letter to Barbara Rollins, Director of Customer
Relations on 2/27/89.

PORTNOY'S FACT FORM (SIDE TWO)

Step 4. Name/Contact	Title/Company	Comments/Action/Date
(Upon completion, proceed to side one, Step 5)		
Randy Shore	Manager at Airport	Telephoned Mr. S. on 2/21 at 415-555-1234. Offered no assistance.
Randy Shore	Manager at Airport	Face-to-face on 2/23. Unwilling to offer reduced charge.
Barbara Rollins	Director of Customer Relations, Courtesy Rent-A-Car	Called Ms. R. on 2/25/89. She promised to review the case.

February 27, 1989

Barbara Rollins
Director, Customer Relations
Courtesy Rent-A-Car
100 3rd Street
Los Angeles, CA 90020

Re: Car Rental, San Francisco Airport, Contract No. 104023; 2/21/89–2/23/89.

Dear Ms. Rollins:

As per our telephone conversation on 2/25/89, I am writing in order to restate what occurred. On 2/21/89 I rented a Ford Taurus station wagon from your San Francisco Airport facility. The contract number was 104023.

Unfortunately, the rear tailgate on the station wagon would not open and I was unable to get full use of the automobile. I was using it to move my belongings from one location to another. When I discovered the problem, I contacted the airport office manager, Randy Shore. This was on 2/21/89. Mr. Shore told me there was nothing he could do about my situation. There were no other station wagons available. I would have to make do.

I used the car for three days. When I returned it on 2/23/89, I asked Mr. Shore not to charge me the station wagon rate, because due to the problem, I was unable to use it as a station wagon. He refused to accommodate me.

In light of my unsuccessful effort to resolve the problem with Mr. Shore, I am contacting you to obtain at least a partial credit for the unsatisfactory operating condition of the automobile I rented. Further, I thought you would want to know how customers are treated at your San Francisco Airport location.

I can be reached at (201)555-1234 during the day and (201)666-4321 in the evenings. A good time to get me is 11:00 A.M. Many thanks in advance for your time and cooperation.

Sincerely,

J. Elias Portnoy

PORTNOY'S FACT FORM (SIDE ONE)

Step 1. Product or Service Information
Retro Cassette-Recorder; Model #RA4600; Serial #56789276B
Purchased 4/10/89 from Peter's Electronics, Orange, N.J.

Step 2. Problem Statement
Volume control malfunction; unable to adjust volume level except very low or very loud.

Step 3. Desired Solution
(Proceed to side two, Step 4)
Product repair or replacement or full refund

Step 5. Actual Solution/Confirmation Communication–Date
Replacement of unit, old one returned to Retro 5/14/89.
Confirmation letter sent 5/14/89.

PORTNOY'S FACT FORM (SIDE TWO)

Step 4. Name/Contact	Title/Company	Comments/Action/Date
(Upon completion, proceed to side one, Step 5)		
Mark Roth	Salesman, Peter's Electronics	Face-to-face on 5/6/89; referred me to store owner.
Saul Maslow	Owner, Peter's Electronics	Telephoned him at 201-555-1234 on 5/12/89. Would not replace or fix or refund.
Ellen Porter	Customer Service Rep., Retro Electronics, Inc.	Telephoned her at 609-555-1234 on 5/12/89. Said she would review with Margaret Josephs, Customer Service Director. Ellen P. called back to say that Margaret J. agreed to replace unit; I have to send back old unit.
Margaret Josephs	Director, Customer Service, Retro Electronics, Inc.	I sent confirmation letter on 5/14/89, detailing our agreement.

May 14, 1989

Ms. Margaret Josephs
Director, Customer Service
Retro Electronics, Inc.
Berlin, NJ 08009

Re: Malfunctioning Cassette-Recorder Volume Control

Dear Ms. Josephs:

As per our telephone conversation today, this letter confirms Retro Electronics' agreement to replace my cassette-recorder, Model RA4600, serial number 56789276B. As agreed, I will send back my malfunctioning unit to you under separate cover.

As we discussed, I was unable to get Peter's Electronics, Orange, NJ, to satisfactorily repair or replace the recorder or refund my money. The volume control does not allow for gradual adjustment of the sound. It is either low or very loud.

I appreciate your assistance on this matter and am very pleased Retro Electronics stands behind its products. I will be inclined to purchase other products made by Retro in the future.

If any additional questions should arise, I can be reached at (201) 555-1234 during the day.

Thank you again for your help.

Sincerely,

J. Elias Portnoy

PORTNOY'S FACT FORM (SIDE ONE)

Step 1. Product or Service Information
HAC Refrigerator; Model #2341Q; Serial #B1234567A
Purchased from Robert's Appliances, Alta Loma, California
Purchased 6/1/89 at a cost of $750.00

Step 2. Problem Statement
Double doors on refrigerator and single door of freezer compartment won't close properly. Cold air escapes, preventing unit from performing normally or efficiently.

Step 3. Desired Solution
(Proceed to side two, Step 4)
Repair unit once and for all, or provide no-cost replacement

Step 5. Actual Solution/Confirmation Communication–Date
Manufacturer's technician replaced double doors and single freezer door completely on 8/2/89.

PORTNOY'S FACT FORM (SIDE TWO)

Step 4. Name/Contact	Title/Company	Comments/Action/Date
(Upon completion, proceed to side one, Step 5)		
Peter Small	Salesman, Robert's Appliances	Contacted on 6/10/89. Referred me to Sam R., store owner.
Sam Roberts	Owner, Robert's Appliances	Contacted by phone 6/10/89 at 555-4321. Promised to send a repairman. A repairman came on 6/12/89 and fixed defective gaskets, but the problem developed again.
Sam Roberts	" "	Telephoned him on 6/25/89 to tell him that the problem has reoccurred. He said he could not help me.
Ellen Ross	Customer Service Rep., Home Appliance Corp. of America, Kansas City, MO.	Telephoned on 6/26/89. She said she would arrange corporate technical service visit. I called again on 7/8/89; 7/11/89; 7/15/89. Spoke with reps. Sue Able and Maria Pride, who both promised to forward my message.
Robert V. Underwood	President, Home Appliance Corp.	Sent letter on 7/20/89. Mr. Underwood's secretary called to arrange for 8/2/89 visit of manufacturer's technician.

July 20, 1989

Robert V. Underwood
President
Home Appliance Corp. of America
Kansas City, MO

Re: Improperly closing doors on HAC Refrigerator Model 2341Q

Dear Mr. Underwood:

I purchased a HAC refrigerator, Model 2341Q, Serial Number B234567A, from Robert's Appliances, Alta Loma, California, on 6/1/89. Within a week of delivery, I found that both the double doors on the refrigerator portion and the single door of the freezer compartment would not stay closed completely. This allows cold air to escape from the unit, preventing the unit from operating normally and efficiently.

I contacted Peter Small, my salesman at Robert's Appliances, and in turn Sam Roberts, the store's owner, concerning this problem on 6/10/89. They sent a repairman to my home that day who identified the door gaskets as defective and replaced them on all doors. The problem developed again two weeks later and Mr. Roberts told me on 6/25 there was nothing else he could or would do to resolve my problem.

I contacted Ellen Ross at your customer service department on 6/26 and she told me that she would arrange for a corporate technical service person to come to my home to evaluate the problem. I have not heard from her to date, and I have tried to contact her three times since 6/26, on 7/4, 7/11, and 7/15, to no avail. Two other customer service representatives I spoke to, Sue Able and Maria Pride, told me they would forward my messages to Ms. Ross.

I am writing to you, Mr. Underwood, because I am dissatisfied with the quality of my refrigerator, am unable to get my retailer to satisfactorily repair the unit and am finding your customer service department unresponsive to my needs.

In light of the expense of this refrigerator, $750, and your company's fine reputation and advertised commitment to customer satisfaction, I would like you to personally arrange for the proper service professional to repair the unit or arrange for a no-cost replacement.

I can be reached at (203)555-1234 days.

I look forward to hearing from you.

Sincerely,

J. Elias Portnoy

▪ ▪ ▪

The Fair Credit Billing Act, which went into effect in 1975, provides consumers with real firepower against a host of grievances. This federal statute offers you protection in any transaction in which you pay by credit card.

If you've been billed incorrectly, double-billed, or billed for someone else's sale; if mail order merchandise doesn't arrive within the specified time period, doesn't arrive at all, or you decide to return the merchandise but are billed anyway; if you are the victim of fraud, inferior workmanship, padded bills, or unnecessary repairs—don't despair. As long as you paid by credit card, all you have to do is contact the card issuer within two billing cycles—sixty days—and they will help you with your problem.

The key is that you have to contact your credit card company in writing, and only in writing. You must send your letter by registered, certified, or overnight mail, return receipt requested. If you've returned merchandise (as when Vickie W. returned the vacation certificates), you must mail it the same way and include a copy of the return receipt. Credit card companies require written documentation and proof of your actions.

The address of where to send your letter is on the back of your monthly bill. If for some reason you cannot find the address there, call the customer service number on your bill and they will tell you.

Using the Fact Form, you can easily identify the information the credit card company needs to act in your behalf. The credit card company will withhold payment to the company in question while they are investigating your problem. In cases where the vendor has already been paid, they will temporarily recredit your account while the investigation is being conducted. If they find in your favor, the credit will stand and they will permanently deduct the amount from your balance, if necessary. If the company wins, credit will be rescinded.

So remember: Pay by credit card whenever possible. Then, if you have a problem, invoke your legal rights via the Fair Credit Billing Act by notifying your credit card company in writing within sixty days.

▪ ▪ ▪

8

.

Working the Tools in Combination

■

STATEMENT OF PHILOSOPHY

The three tools—face-to-face, telephone, and letter writing—are meant to be used in combination. They are interactive. Used interactively, they form an action plan. This action plan draws its strength from the power of facts, a knowledge of human psychology, and experience with the way business works. When brought to bear on a problem encountered in the marketplace, the action plan achieves extremely rewarding results.

There are no appropriate negative anecdotes with which to lead off this short chapter. The reason is that when myself or others have used the tools in combination as an action plan, good things have almost always happened. If we didn't obtain exactly the solution we desired, we came pretty darn close.

For my own part, in the last several years the only times my action plan had been brought to a dead stop was when I had run into truly bad apples—companies that were fraudulent, dishonest, or blatantly, gleefully contemptuous of their customers and reputation. Each of these cases—involving a real-estate agency, a Northern European luxury-goods manufacturer, a small retail concern, and in one particularly galling case, a travel agency—was pursued to a higher authority. With the exception of the European manufacturer, different authorities investigated, prosecuted, and in one case, closed down an exploitative business. Though I lost my money, I at least got the satisfaction of helping to cause a little trouble for a couple of crooks.

As you read through the next chapters, you will become increasingly aware of how to apply the action plan to different situations. Also, the tips and specific nuggets of information about each industry will save you from having all sorts of problems in the first place.

The point is to save money and time and energy, while sparing yourself a great deal of unwanted feelings and awful experience.

When you actually tackle your first problem, you may want to virtually copy the sample letters right out of the book and read from the sample telephone conversations verbatim. Fine. The great thing about this action plan is that once you've worked with it a bit, it starts to feel natural. Get a couple of successes under your belt and you'll find yourself telling people how to take care of their problems with an illiterate word processor or a cruise line that won't admit that thieves are probably wearing your suits.

In any event, the action grid that follows is just to remind you what-to-do-when in the broadest sense. I think you'll be surprised how quickly it too becomes something that you just plain know. (For a good example of how to use all the tools in combination, check chapter 13: Consumer Products.)

TOOL SELECTION ACTION GRID

Face-to-Face	Telephone	Letter Writing
(Return to the point of purchase or source whenever possible)	• Nonportable Products —Major Household Appliances —Furniture —Heavy Equipment	• Persistent Billing/Credit Disputes

• Portable Products
  Personal Items
  (Cosmetics,
  Jewelry, etc.)
	• Services
	  At-Home Repairs
	  Billing Problems, Hotels,
	  Car Rentals,
	  Utility
	  Companies, etc.
	  Banking/Financial
	  Matters
		• High Ticket Items
		—Automobiles
		—Boats
		  Houses

• Small Appliances		• Confirmation of Telephone Agreements
• Product Service Repair		
• Automotive Repair	• Direct Mail Purchases	• Communication with Media Other Authority Resources
• Airline Refunds/Tickets Reissue	• Nontangibles —Insurance	• Document Complicated Facts
• Accidental Occurances (e.g., waiter stains your suit)		• Resolve a Recurring Problem —Service Repair Problem
		• *Optional:* a means of communicating thanks to helpful people

• IF NOT RESOLVABLE PROCEED TO ———▶

• FACE-TO-FACE ITEMS THAT ARE NOT RESOLVABLE
• IF NOT RESOLVABLE PROCEED TO ———▶

• FACE-TO-FACE AND TELEPHONE ITEMS THAT HAVE NOT BEEN RESOLVED

• IF NOT EASILY RESOLVABLE MOVE BACK TO TELEPHONE

◀———

• TELEPHONE USED TO FOLLOW UP ON UNANSWERED LETTERS ———▶

• THEN REPEAT LETTER WRITING FOR CONFIRMATION

9.
Insurance

■

STATEMENT OF PHILOSOPHY

Just because you have some kind of personal relationship with your insurance broker, automatically trusting
him or her may very probably cost you money.

• When Robert R. and family relocated to the Los Angeles
area, Robert joined a country club. Soon thereafter he met
Peter W., a brassy insurance broker who played golf with the
same handicap and enjoyed a little wager on the side also. It
wasn't long before Peter became Robert's insurance broker.

A couple of years later, Robert's oldest child, Pam, turned
sixteen, which, to suburban children, means driving age. Robert called Peter to notify him that Pam should be included in
the family auto policy.

Weeks later, Pam fishtailed on a wet road and slammed into

another car. Both cars were badly damaged. Robert called Peter to report the accident and tell him he could expect to hear from the other party's insurance company. The response he got was like getting struck in the back of the head with a golf ball. "Thank God Pam's okay, but I was waiting to put her on your policy until you told me she had finished driver's ed."

Unable to prove negligence, Robert wound up being responsible for all the damages involved to the tune of several thousand dollars.

One lawyer who profits nicely from situations like this says, "Cases like these are extremely common. Consumers take a casual, easygoing attitude toward insurance-related matters. They spend more time deciding whether to buy something for twenty bucks than they do attending to their insurance where tens of thousands of dollars may be at stake."

• Nancy P. shipped a four-thousand-dollar piece of ceramic sculpture from her home in New Jersey to her son Kip in Miami. The piece left looking like a pair of amorous pheasants, but arrived looking like a couple of Perdue Ovenstuffers. Assuming the work of art to be insured under the fine-arts portion of her homeowners' policy, Nancy called her broker, Todd M.

Todd had inherited the account from his father, who had passed away around the same time as Nancy's husband. To her surprise, Todd barely heard Nancy out before he insisted the fault lay with the shipper because the damage "obviously" occurred en route. "Contact the shipper," he advised.

But the shipper denied responsibility, claiming that the damage was due to improper packaging and, therefore, was a matter between her and her insurance company.

Three times Nancy went back and forth between Todd and the shipper. Then, feeling worn down, she gave up completely.

As one insurance broker commented, "Different business parties will sometimes attempt to shift blame back and forth like a shuttlecock. A good broker, one who is interested in a client's welfare from a long-term standpoint, will, at the very least, walk them through the avenues of recourse to help them recoup their loss. I don't like to think how many brokers are only interested in protecting their short-term bottom line."

• Their great glassy Hamptons summer house was about to be opened. Before it was, however, Norman G. was informed by the maintenance company servicing his pool that when they removed the spring-loaded cover, they found that the pool's vinyl liner had been ruined by some animal. In order to make the pool usable, the entire liner would have to be replaced. According to the maintenance man, the only indigenous animal powerful enough to have done such damage was a raccoon.

Norman called his insurance broker, Frank W., a longtime Hamptons resident and occasional social acquaintance, who had, in fact, had cocktails around the very same pool. Reviewing the policy, Arthur indicated that in order to collect, they would have to prove that damage had been done by a nondomesticated creature. Norman repeated what the pool man had said about a raccoon, to which Frank replied, "Couldn't it have been an exceptionally hungry squirrel, which are considered domesticated? Or, for that matter, a big dog?"

"Look, Frank, there's no such thing as Super Squirrel, and the dogs around here are too well fed to go chomping on vinyl liner."

Frank backed off, saying that all he meant was his company was very careful in cases like these, so he would have to conduct a little investigation.

Apparently Frank's sleuthing did not turn up compelling evidence in Norman's favor: The insurance company refused payment, citing the technicality that there was insufficient proof that the culprit was nondomesticated.

Cases like these lend themselves to humor as long as you're not the victim. Said a lawyer who specializes in insurance problems: "To the unwary, brokers often represent the parent company as tight and difficult. They throw quasi-legitimate technicalities at the wall until one of them sticks. Then they don't have to file a claim."

• Driving in the right-hand lane on a Chicago expressway, Paul K. was passed by a car driving illegally in the breakdown lane to his right. Before he could react, the other car veered into Paul's lane, smashing his front end. The driver of the renegade car, a big dude by the name of Wayne, was plainly high as a kite. Miraculously, his vehicle was hardly damaged. Also miraculously, by the time the police arrived a short while later, Wayne had straightened up. The police report did not indicate fault.

Paul got in touch with his insurance agent, Bruce, who was his wife's cousin. He described the accident and instructed Bruce to process for damages from Wayne's insurance company.

Months passed. Paul went ahead and had his car repaired under the assumption that he would be reimbursed by his insurance company once they'd collected from Wayne's. "Where's the check, Bruce?" became his frustrating refrain.

Then, when he noted a rate hike on his auto insurance bill, he called Bruce again. What he found out sent him ballistic. He learned that based upon entirely false information provided by Wayne, Wayne himself had received thousands of dollars for damages, not only to his car, but to his person. It boggled Paul's mind that his own agent had authorized payment without consulting him and in direct contradiction to the information he had provided.

Said one industry analyst: "You'd be surprised how typical it is for brokers to do things behind their clients' backs that are clearly not in their clients' best interests. Consumers who aren't vigilant, who don't stay right on top of a problem once it occurs, too often discover when it's too late that somebody else's initiative has pulled the rug right out from under their legitimate position."

The advertising jingles and slogans would have you believe that insurance companies are caring, protective, even country-cordial: "You're in good hands with . . . ," "Own a piece of the rock," ". . . I'm glad I metcha." Buy insurance and it's like getting King Kong, Donald Trump, and Dolly Parton squarely in your corner.

The reality can be very different. To begin with, most insurance companies won't deal with consumers directly. The majority of personal insurance is sold by representatives—brokers or agents who are, in fact, independent business people. This would be simple and straightforward, perhaps, were it not for the weird, mystical nature of insurance itself.

Insurance is a unique product. It is not a tangible entity. What you're buying is psychological well-being—peace of mind. The transaction goes as follows: You pay out a considerable sum of money, and in return, you get a promise—if some mishap or disaster should befall you, or your property or belongings, you will receive reimbursement according to how much you've paid out for your loss or pain.

Suppose my living-room lamp blows and sets the rug on fire? Or some maniac sideswipes my car while I'm getting a haircut? What happens if a visitor slips on a grease spot in my kitchen? Or the neighbor's crazy kid who zooms around at warp speed should zoom through my porch's glass door?

Without being paranoid about it, there are an unimaginable variety of rotten, awful, unlucky things that can happen to each and every one of us, most of which, most of the time, are entirely outside our control. So it's not surprising that in order to accommodate the vast number of potential bummers, there is an almost correspondingly wide variety of policies offered. Which, of course, makes buying insurance a highly complex and intimidating proposition. Who can make sense of it? Who can figure out what's best for you?

Brokers can, that's who.

And is it any wonder that with such an abstract, mysterious, complicated product, the vast majority of consumers gravitate to someone with whom they feel they have some kind of personal relationship? In other words, most people pick a particular broker, not a particular insurance company. No matter how distant their relationship with the broker they choose, the fact that the selection is made on a personal basis provides a sense of security. Sure, brokers have got to make a living just like everybody else, but since they know you and you know them, since there's some kind of real connection between you, you rely upon them to first give you the best protection at the lowest price, and then, when something bad happens, redeem your absolute faith in them by fulfilling the promise made to you each time you paid your money.

Why is it, then, that statistics show that one out of three consumers have had insurance problems wherein they never received what they believed they were entitled to? In general, these same people aren't so much angry as they are baffled. If they blame anyone, they blame themselves. When outrageous life situations confronted them in the forms of ravenous raccoons or lying substance abusers, they assumed their interests were being looked out for by their brokers. This assumption—which is really a misconception—costs them money—lots of it.

The reason I was able to discover the way insurance works is because when something suspicious happened to my insurance, I automatically put my action plan into operation. Since the plan is adaptable to all businesses and circumstances, the outcome was positive. Had the consumers in the previous anecdotes known of and used the plan, they too would likely have been rewarded with positive results.

My case began when I purchased a new car, a car slightly more expensive than my last one. To my surprise, when I renewed my policy, the bill registered a whopping increase in my premium. I wasn't asking for a lower deductible, I wasn't asking for coverage different than I'd had before. Yet the insurance company was asking me for seven hundred more dollars—an increase of 35 percent.

I called my broker, a rep from a major insurance company, who had been a college fraternity brother of my father's and had remained a close family friend. I stated my facts: that my new car fell into the same insurance classification; that I deserved preferred status based on an excellent driving record; that I'd never made a claim against the company. Then, I delivered my problem statement—that my premium had been raised by 35 percent; and my desired solution—that I pay the same premium, or if I got a reasonable explanation, a slightly higher one. I anticipated him saying sorry, it must be a mistake, probably a clerical error. He said: I'll investigate.

He called back to tell me that the rate hike was on account of a speeding ticket. But that was six years ago, I said. And I know that according to the law in the state of New York (where I live), the validity of the ticket expired three years ago. He conceded the point. Yet he still insisted there was no recourse except to pay up.

The fellow was too old and close a family friend for me to smell a rat. But I did sense something fishy was going on. So I decided to put my plan to work and seek a solution inside the corporation itself. I realized this might be trickier than usual because insurance companies are especially notorious for having formidable corporate shells.

I began by calling an 800 number I got from my premium statement. I had my Fact Form, a glass of water, and a pen next to me. I reminded myself to be unemotional, brief, concise, and tenacious. I also reminded myself that every call had two purposes: to either get resolve or to get in touch with someone who could give me one.

As I proceeded up the corporate ladder—or, more precisely in this case, through the corporate maze—I kept documentation of every call, got the name and title of everyone I talked to, made a short notation of what they said, and used the accumulating facts to build a power base.

In less than one hour, after bouncing around three departments in different locations, talking to a variety of middle- and upper-level people, I was finally connected with a vice president at the corporate headquarters in Connecticut.

Once again I repeated my story. I could tell he was impressed by my approach, but at the same time felt required to remain protective of what he referred to as his broker's domain. So I asked him directly if he had the authority to make a decision regarding my case. When there was no answer, I persisted, appealing to him not as a corporate player, but as a fellow consumer. Turn your desk around, I asked him, evaluate the facts from my point of view. What would you feel if you were in my position? How would you handle it?

There was a long pause. Then, bingo!

He revealed an industry secret, a closely guarded secret maintained at great cost and unfairness to consumers. What he told me was that although brokers are trained to establish personal relations with their clients, they really function just like salespeople in many other businesses—meaning, they work on commission and have profitability quotas. In the case of the insurance business, the quotas are determined by rationing the amount of insurance sold against the amount of claims processed and paid out. In turn, this ratio determines the types of policies the broker is eligible to sell in any given time period. The consumer, without knowing it, and through absolutely no fault of his or her own, is at the mercy of the individual broker's good or bad luck vis-à-vis his clients. Thus, the merits of our particular circumstances may be irrelevant, for we are forced to exist in the broker's risk pool.

I asked the VP what recourse I had.

"Call other company reps, present your story as you did to me, then ask point-blank whether they are in a position to write you the policy you deserve." He even provided me with the code number of the preferred policy I was seeking.

All the brokers I spoke with were thrown for a loop by my approach. Eventually, I was able to find one who wrote me the policy I was entitled to. Over the short term I saved $700. Over the long term, the utilization of my action plan will save me many thousands.

What I learned from this and succeeding experiences with insurance was:

1.   When purchasing insurance, sit down and have a heart-to-heart talk with your broker. Be perfectly explicit from the outset as to exactly what coverage you think you need.

2.   Don't be afraid to obtain what amounts to a second opinion from other brokers representing the same insurance company. (Contact the corporate headquarters of your insurance company to obtain a list of the other brokers in your home area.)

3.   Once you've gotten a policy, make sure you understand exactly what it is you are paying for. Ask a lot of questions.

4.   Realize that no matter what kind of personal relationship you have with your broker, when it comes to business, you are involved in a typical buyer-seller relationship. This is not distrust; it is the realistic recognition that business is by nature adversarial.

5.   Do not automatically trust; keep your guard up; do not simply rely on your broker to take care of you; monitor your policy closely; question even a 5 percent rate hike.

6.   If you get persistently fuzzy explanations, switch brokers.

7.   If you have any doubt that you are not getting what you think you are entitled to, use the action plan to get what you deserve.

PORTNOY'S FACT FORM (SIDE ONE)

Step 1. Product or Service Information
ADI Auto Insurance Policy for a 1987 BMW 4-door sedan
Broker, Jack Collins, Collins Insurance, Garden City, New
York

Step 2. Problem Statement
Policy overcharge by original broker, Jack Collins.

Step 3. Desired Solution
Adjusted (lower) policy rate for same coverage

Step 5. Actual Solution/Confirmation Communication–Date
Policy reassigned to new broker recommended by ADI. Significant rate adjustment obtained for same coverage. Thank-
you note sent to Arnold Wilson, 11/24/88.

PORTNOY'S FACT FORM (SIDE TWO)

Step 4. Name/Contact	Title/Company	Comments/Action/Date
Mary Ross	Customer Service Rep, ADI, Hartford, CT, via 800 number on premium notice	Referred to Mrs. Robinson, supervisor in New Haven office who handles some NY-based customers (203-555-5400) on 11/21/88.
Roberta Robinson	Supervisor, Customer Service, New Haven office	Referred to Robin Stevens, Elmira, NY, corporate office, Director of Customer Service for NY accounts (212-555-5555) on 11/21/88.
Robin Stevens	Director, Customer Service, Elmira, NY, office	Stevens contacted Jeff Peterson, VP, Customer Service, Elmira, NY, office to determine best course of action. Referred to Arnold Wilson, VP, Broker Relations. 11/21/88
Arnold Wilson	VP, Broker Relations, Elmira, NY, office	Recommends local broker, Joseph, Edwards and Marks. Provides policy account information to obtain proper preferred customer policy rate (SY code). Recommends that Joseph, Edwards and Marks become my "servicing" agent on old policy until it expires. 11/21/88

SAMPLE TELEPHONE CONVERATION
The Insurance Issue

If you have an insurance problem you can't satisfactorily resolve with your broker, don't automatically trust him and let it go at that. Instead, use the phone to get what you deserve. Hold the phone in one hand and follow the script held in your other hand.

STEP ONE:
The first call: My initial corporate contact; an 800 number indicated on my premium notice

Always ask for customer service first. Almost every company has some form of one.

A: ADI.

P: Yes, hello, can you connect me with your customer service department?

A: What is your problem?

Now state your problem.

P: I have received what I believe to be misinformation about my ADI auto insurance policy from my broker, and I need to speak to someone in customer service.

A: I will connect you.

P: Thank you.

A: Customer service, Mary Ross speaking.

Your first key contact. Keep notes and use the individual's name immediately in your conversation. This creates a bond right away.

P: Yes, Mary, this is Mr. Portnoy. I am an ADI customer and I feel my broker is overcharging me for auto insurance for my new car, and I want to check with someone in corporate about how I might go about resolving this issue.

A: What exactly is the problem?

*State the Facts
State the Problem
State the Desired
Solution, plus appeal
for assistance.*

P: I recently purchased a new car to replace my old one and when I contacted my broker to adjust my insurance policy to cover this new car, he told me that my premium would increase $700.

When I inquired why I was being charged so much more money for a car that was in the same classification as my old car, my broker told me that my record still showed a speeding ticket from six years ago. I told him and he agreed that such a traffic violation only remains active on your record for three years and therefore could not be legally used to raise my rates. When I asked him to make the appropriate adjustment, he told me he couldn't do it and that was that. Ms. Ross, I would like to stay with ADI and I know I am entitled to a preferred customer rate. *I need your help* to find out what I can do to get a reduction in my premium.

A: Mr. Portnoy, what state is your car registered in?

P: New York.

A: I see. Well, I cannot help you from this office and I am not sure exactly what to tell you.

Restate what you are seeking, keeping in mind that in order to get what you want you must reach someone with the authority to make a decision.

P: Who can you refer me to that can check my record and help me obtain the preferred rate?

A: I suggest you call a Mrs. Robinson. She is a supervisor in our Hartford office. I think she handles New York accounts. Her number is 555-5555.

Always be polite. So many people forget how important a simple "thank you" is.

P: Thank you very much. I really appreciate your help.

A: I hope you get your problem resolved.

STEP TWO:
Mrs. Robinson, Supervisor

A: Roberta Robinson.

Use the name of your first contact as a stepping-stone or bridge.

P: Yes, Mrs. Robinson, Ms. Ross in your other Hartford office referred me to you and said you might be able to help me resolve my dilemma.

A: I will try. What seems to be the problem?

Each time you restate your problem it will be easier and sound more natural.

P: I am a New York customer of ADI for my auto insurance. Quite simply, my broker has admittedly overcharged me on the insurance for my new car and he will not adjust my premium to reflect the fact that I deserve a preferred rate status. He is using the excuse of an old speeding ticket which expired three years ago to explain a $700 increase in my insurance. Can you check my record and help me obtain the rate I am entitled to?

A: I am afraid I cannot do that. You see we do not deal directly with the public. We deal only with insurance brokers.

Give a nudge disguised as a helpful offering.

P: I realize that. But I think you can see that I have reason not to trust my broker any longer and that *I would* *hope that ADI corporate would like to know that one of its brokers may be misrepresenting the company to the public.*

A: I do not have the authority to check your records, nor am I sure that there is anything that you can do about your situation. But your situation does sound like it warrants attention.

Create empathy: Have them put themselves in your place. Encourage listener to direct you to a decision maker.

P: Mrs. Robinson, what would you do if you were me? Is there some individual who has the authority to investigate my case?

A: I really don't know. Maybe you should contact our corporate office in Elmira, New York, and ask for Robin Stevens. She is Director of Customer Service for New York accounts. Her number is 555-5555.

P: Thank you for your time.

A: You're welcome.

STEP THREE:
Robin Stevens, Director

A: Ms. Stevens' office.

*Mention your contacts;
contacts get you
through secretaries,
assistants, receptionists.
Contacts open doors.
Use the Ms. pronoun
for women in business
unless they have
referred to themselves
differently.*

P: This is Eli Portnoy. I have spoken with Mary Ross and most recently with Roberta Robinson in your Hartford office. Mrs. Robinson referred me to Ms. Stevens. Is she in, please?

A: What is this in reference to?

*Flatter the corporate
player by telling her
she has the authority to
help you resolve your
problem.*

P: Mrs. Robinson has directed me to Ms. Stevens to resolve a problem I am having with my auto insurance broker who represents ADI in New York State. *Mrs. Robinson told me that Ms. Stevens is a director with the authority to resolve my problem.*

A: Just a minute, please.

P: Thank you.

A: Robin Stevens.

P: Yes, Ms. Stevens. *I hope you can help me. I have talked to Mary Ross* *and Roberta Robinson in Hartford and I have been told that you have the authority to investigate and resolve my problem.*

A: How can I be of assistance?

Restate your case.

P: *Here are the facts.* I am a New York ADI auto insurance customer. My broker is Jack Collins in Garden City, New York. Mr. Collins has acknowledged that he is charging me over $700 more than I should have to pay for auto insurance. That is, he is not giving me the preferred rate I am entitled to on my new car because he claims a six-year-old speeding ticket accidentally remained on my record. Further, he has stated that he can do nothing about this error and I am obligated to pay for his error. I want you to correct my records at the corporate level and reduce my premium to the proper rate.

A: Is this a new policy with ADI?

P: No. This is an adjusted policy to cover a new car that is in the same classification as the previous one.

A: When does your present policy expire?

P: In four months.

A: There really is nothing we can do. We do not handle consumers directly and I cannot override the broker's policy.

Here you must create empathy.

P: Ms. Stevens, *what should I do?* I obviously don't want to pay the extra $700 since I know that I really am not required to do so. Yet if I don't, you'll drop my insurance. And I don't want to have to change insurance companies in the middle of my policy since I will forfeit the money I have already paid.

A: That's correct.

Pursue role reversal. Take the corporate player out of his/her office frame of reference.

P: Isn't there anything I can do? *Place yourself in my shoes and think about being asked to pay for someone else's mistake.*

A: I understand your problem and if what you say is true, then it is quite unfortunate.

P: There must be an individual or group that reviews broker-related complaints.

A: Can you hold a minute? I want to chat with Jeff Peterson, one of our VPs, about this matter.

P: Yes, thank you, I will hold.

A: Mr. Portnoy, Mr. Peterson suggests you call Arnold Wilson, another one of our vice presidents. He thinks

Mr. Wilson may be able to help in some way.

P: I appreciate your efforts.

A: You are welcome. Good luck.

P: Thank you very much.

STEP FOUR:
Mr. Wilson, VP

Make sure your Fact Form reflects all your contacts to this point.

A: Mr. Wilson's office.

P: Yes, this is Mr. Portnoy. I am an ADI customer. I have spoken with Mary Ross and Roberta Robinson in your other Hartford office and then I was referred to Mr. Wilson by his associates Jeff Peterson and Robin Stevens in this office.

A: What is this in reference to?

P: Mr. Peterson and Ms. Stevens feel that Mr. Wilson can resolve a problem I am having with one of your brokers.

A: Let me see if he is available.

A: Wilson.

P: Yes, Mr. Wilson. Thank you for taking my call. I have just finished talking with Robin Stevens and she and Jeff Peterson both feel you can resolve a problem I have with my ADI auto policy.

A: What seems to be the problem?

You have told the story so many times it's driving you crazy, but this listener has not heard it before.

P: Jack Collins of Collins' Insurance in Garden City is my broker and handles my auto insurance policy with your company. I have known Jack for many years, since he is a fraternity brother of my father's. However, I feel that Mr. Collins is not handling my account in a professional manner. Specifically, I recently bought a new car, although one in the same car classification as my previous car. Mr. Collins told me my premium would be $700 more than the previous one. I asked him why the new premium should cost so much more and he told me he accidentally left a six-year-old speeding ticket on my record. He acknowledged it had expired three years ago and legally should have no bearing on my rate. However, he said the policy has been written and there is nothing he can do about it. I asked him to reimburse me the difference since it was his error. But he refused. So I decided to pursue a solution myself.

A: Mr. Portnoy, since the policy has already been written there is nothing you can do unless you want to change insurance companies. I also don't think I really can comment on Mr. Collins' actions. I do not know Mr. Collins.

More importantly, we do not write policies, brokers do, as I am sure you know. Therefore, I cannot correct or adjust your policy. We only deal with brokers. It is my responsibility to protect our brokers' domain.

Do not threaten. But infer the possibility of this being a matter for a higher authority. Do so in the form of concern for the company's reputation.

P: Mr. Wilson, I appreciate that you do not write policies, but surely this is not the first time an ADI customer has contacted you directly about a problem with a broker. *But the key issue as I see it, and the reason why I think you would want to get involved, is that this broker represents your company and given these facts it could be construed that he is acting unethically and that reflects negatively on your company. Don't you agree?*

A: There is really nothing I can do for you.

Time for role reversal.

P: You know, Mr. Wilson, if the increase had been a few dollars I probably would have let it slide, however, since it is such a large amount of money I just could not let the issue pass. *Mr. Wilson, if you were sitting on my side of the desk, how would you handle this? What would you do? Pay it* or fight it? *The facts clearly indicate that the broker is at fault. Would you like me to review them with you again?* [*Pause.*]

I mean, Mr. Wilson, it just seems unreasonable for me to have to pay for Mr. Collins' error. What would you do?

A: Well, I understand your frustration. You could change brokers and maintain your policy with ADI.

P: Is it possible for me to find another ADI agent in the New York area that can revise my policy now and without a penalty?

A: It's possible. You see, Mr. Portnoy, I really shouldn't be telling you this. But it is possible that your present broker's profitability with ADI is not good and therefore he was not able to write you a new policy at the old rate. Even if you were entitled to it.

Breakthrough! You are on your way. Maintain control, and let him tell you everything you need to know. You will be surprised what happens when you let the floodgates open.

P: Could you please explain?

A: Brokers, like other salespeople, are periodically evaluated on their profitability performance. If a broker has had too many clients make claims against their policies in a given time period, and therefore his profitability to the corporation is diminished, he would not be allowed to write the best policies for a period of time. Even if some of his clients are qualified.

P: So that's the reason behind the increase!

A: Well, I am not saying that's the exact reason you got hit with a major increase you did not expect, but it is a possibility.

Probe for more information.

P: How do I go about finding another agent that can write the best policies?

A: I really can't tell you that. I am not in a position to recommend one broker over another.

P: Then why don't you tell me the names of brokers who represent you in the Manhattan area and I will follow up with them on my own. Is there a policy code I should ask for?

A: What are the first two letters of your policy?

P: SX

A: You will want a SY policy; that's the code for preferred customers.

P: I have had an SX policy for a long time. Does that mean I have been overpaying for some time?

A: That's possible. The firm that comes to mind in Manhattan that I know well is Josephs, Edwards and Marks. Just call them and ask for a sales agent and tell them you want them to become a *servicing* agent on your old policy and to write you an SY policy for your new car.

You can never show too much gratitude.

P: A servicing agent, okay. . . . I really appreciate this information, Mr. Wilson. I can't thank you enough for your help.

A: Good luck.

P: Thank you. Thank you very much for your advice.

A: Mr. Portnoy, be sure to send a letter to your present broker notifying him you have selected another agent to service your policy. You will probably be asked to send a copy of that letter to the new firm as well.

P: I will. Thank you again.

24 November 1988

Mr. Arnold Wilson
Vice President, Broker Relations
ADI Insurance Corporation
345 Lakeview Road
Elmira, NY 10039

Re: J. E. Portnoy, auto insurance premium

Dear Mr. Wilson:

Thank you so much for your efforts on my behalf in respect to my problem with my unfairly raised automobile insurance premium. Thanks to your information, I was able to obtain the rate that my circumstances warrant.

It is very reassuring to know that a company like ADI has executives with integrity and discrimination. By standing behind what is fair and just, you showed me that you care about your customers. I plan on remaining a loyal customer of ADI for the foreseeable future. Thank you again.

Sincerely,

J. Elias Portnoy

10

.

Automobiles

Historically, the automobile has been a central part of the American dream, signifying freedom, mobility, and adventure. Today, however, owning a car is not a casual, carefree experience. Ownership requires understanding one's rights, and knowing the options available when something goes—as it usually does—wrong.

• Brian K., a salesman for a large office-supply company, was responsible for covering a territory that included Florida, Georgia, and Alabama. For prestige, Brian always drove a large American sedan. Working the Sunbelt made him especially reliant on its air-conditioning system. Thus, when the system broke down on his two-month-old car, he broiled for ten days before getting it back to the dealer for servicing. As it turned out, that was merely the first in a series of several sweaty tri-state swings: the air conditioning not only broke down repeatedly, it didn't function properly when he needed it most on long drives in brutal heat. The fact that the dealer didn't charge him a penny while the car was under warranty was hardly a consolation.

Then, the car went off warranty and, predictably, the system broke down, causing him to suffer through a six-day swelter. When the dealer estimated that repair would cost $800, the steam building up in Brian's body came out his mouth; he lambasted the dealer, who took it very coolly, and then Brian traded the car in on a brand-new model at a substantial loss.

• Elana S. bought her first car soon after her divorce. She was a novice at the whole business of car ownership because her husband had taken care of all car-related matters. When her Japanese-made car turned "sluggish" after logging only 7,500 miles, Elana took it to the dealer who had sold it to her. Four times over the next three months she returned to the dealer, each time telling the service department that the car's engine "ran rough," and "idled funny." Driving the car was not a pleasant experience. However, the dealer insisted that they could find no problem with either the engine or the car's general performance. Perplexed, Elana decided to bite the bullet. But when things seemed to deteriorate as the car was approaching the end of its warranty, she panicked and sold the "mystery mobile" for as much as she could get.

• As soon as the warranty expired on Dr. James R.'s Detroit-made station wagon, it began to fall apart. First, the driver's side window wouldn't close; then, the heater couldn't be turned off; and finally, the transmission went awry. Not only did the dealer make the doctor wait two weeks to get a service appointment, but the quality of the repair was marginal and the charges sky-high. Fed up, Dr. R. decided that if there was another problem, he'd take the car to the local service station mechanic. It's got to be an improvement, he figured.

Wrong. When the transmission failed a second time, he

took the wagon to the mechanic, who gave him all sorts of assurances about quality workmanship, and mentioned a price that, compared to the dealer's gougings, sounded like a bargain.

Days later the mechanic called to say the car was ready. "Totally repaired and road-tested," he promised. What the mechanic didn't say was that he had discovered several other problems and repaired them as well. The bill was two and a half times more than the doctor had expected it to be. Reluctantly, he paid the bill, with a check, rationalizing that if the car was really in tip-top condition, he wouldn't mind the surprise.

This was only the first surprise. Ten days later the transmission started slipping again, the battery went dead, and a new rattle emanated from the engine compartment. In a fury the doctor called the mechanic, telling him in no uncertain terms to come pick up the car immediately and fix it at no cost. At least the mechanic did pick the car up. After that, things got sticky. He insisted the new problems were unrelated to the original ones and would cost another hefty sum to repair. Another vicious cycle had begun.

Car troubles are one of the most common and upsetting problems experienced by consumers. Besides other matters such as theft, accidents, drunk drivers, and insurance, the problems we're addressing fall into three main categories.

1. Malfunction or defect with a car under warranty that the dealer is unable—or unwilling—to repair satisfactorily.

2. Malfunction or defect with a car no longer under warranty that a dealer is unable to repair satisfactorily.

3. Unsatisfactory repair by an independent service facility (not the manufacturer's authorized dealer).

In the case of number one, consumers like Brian K. and Elana S. have several recourses. If the car under warranty continues to have a problem (or problems), there are the lemon laws (referred to as Auto Repair/Service Regulations in some states). These laws or regulations exist in forty-six states and the District of Columbia. They entitle you to a new car or your money back if, during either the first year in some states or the second year in others, a substantial problem cannot be fixed in a certain number of repair attempts (usually four) or in a certain number of days (usually thirty).

To invoke the lemon law, you have to report your problem in writing to the manufacturer or to one of the manufacturer's dealers. If the manufacturer and the dealer refuse to recognize the problem, or won't offer a replacement or a buy-back, then you have to take your case to one of a number of arbitration programs. These programs are all decidedly cheaper and less time-consuming than filing a lawsuit. In any event, if the results of the arbitration are not satisfactory, you still retain the right to sue.

The arbitration boards run by the states of Connecticut, Florida, Hawaii, Maine, Massachusetts, New York, New Jersey, Texas, Vermont, Washington, and the District of Columbia have obtained a significantly higher percentage of replacements and buy-backs for consumers than Better Business Bureaus or industry-run programs. (Though, in Florida, you are required by law to try the manufacturer's program before pursuing arbitration.)

The way to get arbitration going is by contacting your state attorney general's office, or your state's consumer-protection office. You must be able to supply copies of repair orders, bills, and correspondence. In a number of states there is a filing fee of up to $200, refundable if the case is resolved in your favor.

In many other states, you can arbitrate through programs that are sponsored by voluntarily participating manufacturers.

- The *Autoline* program at 150 Better Business Bureaus arbitrates problems for GM, Honda, Nissan, Volkswagen, Audi, Rolls-Royce, and Saab. Thirteen other manufacturers participate in selected states only. (Check your Better Business Bureau for information.)

- The *Autocap* program (the National Association of Auto Dealers, located at 8400 Westpark Dr., McLean, VA 22102) arbitrates problems for Alfa Romeo, Austin Rover, BMW, Fiat, Honda, Isuzu, Jaguar, Mazda, Mitsubishi, Nissan, Peugeot, Rolls-Royce, Saab, Volvo, and Yugo. Decisions by this program are not binding.
- *Autosolve* (the American Automobile Association, located at 1000 AAA Dr., Heathrow, FL 32746) runs arbitration programs for Toyota and Hyundai.
- *The American Arbitration Association* (140 West 51 Street, New York, NY 10020) runs programs for Mazda, Volvo, Porsche, and Suzuki.
- Chrysler and Ford run their own arbitration programs (details available on your warranty). For information, Chrysler can be reached by calling 313-956-5970. Ford can be reached at 800-241-8450.

It is vital to present your case according to the dictates of the Fact Form. Your opponent—the manufacturer's representative—has a great deal of experience arbitrating cases. Before going into arbitration, it might be wise to call the National Highway Traffic Safety Administration's Office of Technical Reference (202-366-2768) because they might provide technical service bulletins pertaining to your car (if your model is known to have a recurring problem). It is also a good idea to have a qualified mechanic inspect your vehicle, then describe, either in writing or in person at the hearing, what is wrong and why it is the manufacturer's or the dealer's fault.

As to number three—unsatisfactory repair by an independent service facility—bad experiences are many, remedies are few. Unneeded repairs, suddenly emerging "new" problems, padded bills, incompetent work—consumers like Dr. James R. often suffer from not just one of these injustices, but from all of them. In general, state bureaus of motor vehicles, or bureaus of auto repair (which license shops in Michigan and California), or consumer affairs departments are at least capable of mediating problems. However, only a few of them can order refunds, levy fines, or revoke a shop's license.

There are a number of states in which you are protected by law from the kind of "five o'clock surprises" like the ones visited on the good doctor. These laws say that when a shop hits you with repairs not stated on the required estimate, or inflates the charges at the last minute, you don't have to pay. If the shop plays hardball and refuses to release your car until you do, use the Fair Credit Billing Act to your advantage. Pay by credit card, then write the card issuer a letter and proceed accordingly.

It should be noted that three limitations apply whenever you dispute the quality of goods or services you've received, rather than a billing error. One: You have to make a good-faith attempt to resolve your dispute with the shop in question. Two: The shop must be in your home state or within one hundred miles of your home address. Three: The amount in dispute must be greater than $100.

Here are five rules I recommend to all car owners. They are preventive measures, and will save you a lot of grief in a range of possible circumstances.

1. Make absolutely sure that your repair order (or work order) explicitly and specifically identifies your problem. Fill out a Fact Form the way you normally would, then transfer the information onto the repair order. For example, do not write, "The car vibrates sometimes"; write, "At speeds above 55

MPH, the steering wheel vibrates." Vagueness allows others to wriggle free of responsibility.

2. *Insist* that you be taken on a road test with the service adviser or technician *before* and *after* service is done. Do not pay your bill until you have done so.

3. If you have an ongoing problem, make sure the repair order clearly makes mention of each time the problem has arisen. Repair orders, like Fact Forms, should document all your activity.

4. Keep all repair orders and bills for your car in a special file, along with an up-to-date Fact Form.

5. Whenever possible, pay by credit card. Then you can invoke the Fair Credit Billing Act.

This brings us to category number two—malfunction or defect that appears when the car is no longer under warranty—and to the sixth rule. Besides adhering to the rules outlined above, there is one little-known avenue of resolve for some consumers, depending on who their car is made by. I came across this valuable information while pursuing a dispute concerning a car still under warranty.

As a reward for landing a good job—a job that involved considerable driving—I bought myself a beautiful and expensive car. The car was made by German Autos of North America and cost nearly as much as my parents paid for their first home in the mid-fifties. Needless to say, I had great expectations about the car, and so was especially unhappy when it developed a problem within a few months of purchase. The problem was that the exhaust pipe bolted to the undercarriage of the car banged into the center console in the passenger compartment whenever I went over a bump. My unhappiness increased when three separate dealerships refused to recognize that I had a problem. They insisted I was imagining it and would have to learn to "live with it."

So I went into action. I filled out my Fact Form, identifying the car, the model year, the number of miles driven, the date of purchase, and the dealer from whom I made the purchase. I described the problem as: Road bumps cause some part of the undercarriage to bang into the center console in the passenger compartment; unable to get any recognition of the problem from three different dealers (I listed them).

My desired solution was either satisfactory repair or replacement under the state lemon law. I realized that I would have a very tough time winning my case via the lemon law or via arbitration programs because all the dealers had adamantly denied any evidence to support my claim.

I knew my best bet was to use my action plan and go straight to corporate, in this case German Autos of North America. Obtaining the number from my owner's manual, I called and spoke with a very pleasant customer service representative, who told me very pleasantly that she was not allowed to recommend a dealer who might be more likely to help me, and could not see any way the corporation could evaluate my case. She did respond to my telephone techniques, however, and told me the director of customer service would call me back the next day. I did not wait, but was unable to reach the gentleman whose name I had secured.

Anyway, the next day he called. I told my story, adding that the customer service rep had indicated he was the person who could solve my problem. He hedged, asking me whether I'd road tested the car with a service adviser or technician. I told him I'd never thought of doing this—which at that time I hadn't. He suggested I return to the dealer and specifically ask for a road test conducted in this manner.

I told him it took four weeks to get an appointment and I wasn't crazy about waiting anymore. Also, if I did wait, and still didn't get resolve, I'd have to go through the pain of invoking the lemon law (it would be my fourth unsuccessful attempt).

I applied telephone pressure points numbers two and three, asking him whether there might be someone, perhaps the person he reported to, who could expedite the situation. No, he said.

Then I asked him what he would do if he were in my shoes. I told him how much I loved the car and how much cars mattered to me. If you were confronted by just this circumstance, how would you handle it, I asked.

It worked like a charm. He revealed to me that German Autos of North America maintains a regionally based (or zone) technical service staff. They are called "troubleshooters." The existence of these troubleshooters is not advertised or promoted, but they are available to consumers on a priority basis. I asked how to contact my regional rep and he gave me the name. He said the fellow would call me. (I knew that if I was not contacted within forty-eight hours, I would seek the individual out through the corporate operator.) I thanked him profusely.

The troubleshooter called the next day, heard my story, and agreed to meet. Within ten minutes, including a two-minute test drive, he had isolated the problem and got the car into the service bay, where it was repaired, under his supervision, fifteen minutes later. He suggested we road test the car to make sure I was satisfied. We did and I was.

During the road test, I asked him why the dealer hadn't recommended him to begin with, and why the people at GA of NA were reluctant to disclose the information as well. He explained that dealers prefer to handle their own customers themselves, that there is a shortage of troubleshooters, and that manufacturers do not like to "show up" dealers.

He also clued me in to some other very valuable information. He said that all automakers maintain regional offices with customer relations staffs, which might be helpful in some cases. Of the Big Three American automakers, however, only Cadillac, a division of GM, maintains a truly active staff of service technicians—troubleshooters. American automakers consider consumer-oriented programs like the troubleshooters to be prohibitively expensive and not worth the investment. Japanese and European manufacturers, on the other hand, all maintain active staffs. But they do not advertise or promote them. He said, "For consumers like yourself, who present themselves in a nonthreatening manner, and present their problems in an organized manner, the troubleshooter organization is likely to be put at your disposal. *Even if your car is no longer under warranty.*"

A car no longer under warranty will sometimes be "goodwilled" (fixed free of charge or at a very reduced rate) if the troubleshooter is sympathetic to your case. An unemotional demeanor, politeness, accurate documentation, and a clear understanding of one's problem are the elements that win the troubleshooter's favor. Over the last few years, I have used this information to help many people whose cars had gone off warranty.

Rule number six then should read: Before going to arbitration or into a lawsuit, contact the manufacturer directly. Your likelihood of a quick resolve is greatly increased. It is even worthwhile contacting the manufacturer when you have purchased a used car so that recall or other pertinent information can be relayed to you, the car's new owner, directly.

PORTNOY'S FACT FORM (SIDE ONE)

Step 1. Product or Service Information
German Autos of North America
1985 Model Z1000
10,551 miles on it to date
Purchased on 3/1/85
Purchased from Race Imports, Short Island, NY

Step 2. Problem Statement
Road bumps cause some part of the undercarriage—the exhaust pipe?—to ram into the center console of the passenger compartment. Unable to get recognition of problem from three dealers: Race Imports, Short Island, NY/James Reeds, service adviser; Import Motors, Roland, NY/Mike Robinson, service adviser; Marques Motors, Kings, NY/Raymond Keynes, service adviser.

Step 3. Desired Solution
Satisfactory repair or car replacement (lemon law, arbitration, etc.)

Step 5. Actual Solution/Confirmation Communication–Date
Problem resolved with corporate service technician–troubleshooter.
Sent thank-you notes to Alan Visor and Larry Roll, 9/27/85.

PORTNOY'S FACT FORM (SIDE TWO)

Step 4. Name/Contact	Title/Company	Comments/Action/Date
Ellen Devries	Customer Service rep, German Autos of North America (201-555-1234)	Called on 9/21/85. Can't recommend dealer. Alan Visor, Director of Customer Service, will call back.
Alan Visor	Director, Customer Service, German Autos of North America (201-555-1234)	Called on 9/22/85. Recommends corporate technical service rep. Rep to contact me. Name: Larry Roll.
Larry Roll	Regional Service Technician, German Autos of North America (201-555-5353)	Called me on 9/23/85. Made appointment to meet me at Race Imports on Friday 9/26.

▪ ▪ ▪

Consumers have been very well served by two relatively new federal laws relating to the purchase of used cars. One law states that all used cars must post window stickers that divide the cars into two groups: Stickers reading "Sold As Is" mean the used-car dealer is under no obligation whatsoever; stickers reading "Warranty" mean the dealer must abide by the terms of the particular warranty.

The second law requires used-car dealers to allow customers to have an independent mechanic inspect the car prior to purchase. If they balk, consumers may notify the Federal Trade Commission or the Department of Motor Vehicles in their state. Failure to comply with these laws has already caused a number of used-car dealers to lose their licenses.

▪ ▪ ▪

SAMPLE TELEPHONE CONVERSATION
AUTOMOBILES

STEP ONE:
Locate corporate headquarters and telephone number by:
—finding corporate address in owner's manual

—calling local dealer
—obtaining sales brochure from local dealer
—local library reference material

STEP TWO:
Call 800 information for toll-free corporate telephone number. If none exists, call local information for headquarter's telephone number.

Note all the facts and names of contacts on your Fact Form. Tell your story, Product, Problem, and Desired Solution, succinctly.

GA: German Autos of North America.

EP: Customer service, please.

GA: Customer service, Ellen DeVries.

EP: Yes, hello, Ms. DeVries, my name is Eli Portnoy. I own a 1985 1000i, purchased new in March from Race Imports in Short Island, New York. Overall, I am very happy with the vehicle; however, I have experienced difficulties with the undercarriage of the car that three dealers have not been able to repair. It appears the exhaust system is loose and rams up into the passenger compartment when the car travels over road bumps.

I would like someone at the corporate level to examine my car and help me get it properly fixed. I am very unhappy with the dealer's service and would like your help. Can you recommend a dealer who does good work?

GA: Mr. Portnoy, we cannot recommend one dealer over another. What were the other two dealers you took your car to?

EP: Import Motors, Roland, New York, and Marques Motors, Kings, New York.

GA: I see. Well, Mr. Portnoy, let me share this information with Alan Visor, the director of customer service, and he will get back to you.

Find out "when" they will get back to you.

EP: Is he not available now?

GA: No, I am afraid not, but he will get back to you.

EP: When can I expect to hear from Mr. Visor?

GA: Probably tomorrow.

Next Day

GA: Mr. Portnoy, this is Alan Visor of German Autos of North America. I understand you have been having some difficulties with your car. Can you review this with me?

Always thank people for returning your call right away. A pleasantry or a compliment sets the tone of the conversation and tells them you're not starting out hostilely.

EP: Yes, Mr. Visor. Thank you for following up on my call. I own a 1985 1000i, which I purchased new from Race Imports in March. Since delivery, I have experienced a loud thumping noise when driving over road bumps, especially on highways. I feel the problem is related to the exhaust system mount—it may be loose or improperly attached. I have worked with James Reeds at Race Imports several times, and Mike Robinson at Import Motors, and Ray Keynes at Marques Motors.

Be specific about what has been said to you, if you mention it at all.

None of them can find the problem, which has been plaguing me for six months. The dealers make me feel like they are doing me a favor and there's no real problem with the car. Jim Reeds told me that it sounds like the problem is just a reflection of the car's personality on the road. I can't believe that.

I would like someone at the corporate level to examine the car and assist me in getting it repaired to my satisfaction.

GA: I am not sure I can be of help. I cannot recommend a particular dealer. Let me ask you a question. Did any of the dealer's service advisers or technicians road test the car with you?

Corporate player may attempt to side-step your desired result. Listen, but remain committed to your cause.

EP: No. Should they have?

GA: Yes, they should have. Let me make a suggestion. Before we go any further, I think you should contact your original dealer and ask specifically for a road test with a technician. I think you will find that together you will be able to resolve the problem.

EP: Mr. Visor, I didn't know that that kind of service was offered by the dealers during service appointments. After waiting three to four weeks for the appointment, I feel lucky even if they take down any information when I bring the car in for servicing.

GA: Make another appointment with Jim Reeds at Race Imports and see what happens.

EP: Under normal circumstances I might agree to do this. However, this will be the fourth attempt to repair this problem and I am not thrilled about waiting another three to four weeks for an appointment. There must be another option. I am not confident the dealer's service people know what to look for. I would agree to go back if you would call on my behalf to Jim Reeds to set up the appointment more quickly than normal.

GA: No, I can't do that for you.

If the corporate player isn't offering you workable solutions or guidance, a disguised threat—"I understand the laws that protect me"—can go a long way.

It's helpful to take the corporate player out of his corporate shoes and put him into your shoes; empathy is a powerful thing. If necessary, ask the key question more than once and in different ways.

EP: Mr. Visor, I'm sure you realize that if Race Imports fails to repair the problem this time, I am entitled under the lemon law to seek a new car or refund. I would prefer to just get this car running properly; it would be a lot less painful for us both, don't you agree? Is there perhaps someone, a person you report to, who might expedite the situation? I mean, if this were your car wouldn't you agree that this would be the easiest path, or what would you really do if you were in my shoes? Turn the situation around. Look at it for a second from my point of view.

Bingo! You're finally getting corporate-level help.

GA: Well, I do understand your frustration. . . . [*Pause*] I can try to put you in touch with one of our regional corporate service advisers. They handle only extreme problem cases. I can't guarantee anything, but he will arrange to meet you at your dealer and review the problem with both you and the dealer's service staff. That's the best I can do.

Let the corporate player know you're encouraged by his actions.

EP: That sounds like progress. I am sure this can be resolved quickly with help from someone knowledgeable from corporate. How do I contact this person?

Get the facts! Keep control of the flow.

GA: I will contact him for you. He will call you. His name is Larry Roll. Can he reach you at this number?

EP: Yes. When can I expect to hear from him?

GA: In a day or two.

Next Day

GA: Mr. Portnoy, Larry Roll, from German Autos of North America. I understand you are experiencing difficulties with your 1000i.

Follow-up call. Thank you sets the tone.

EP: Yes, Mr. Roll, thank you for following up on my call.

GA: No problem. How can I be of assistance?

EP: I understand from Mr. Visor that you will meet me and my dealer and evaluate the car with their service staff.

GA: Yes, would three P.M. on Friday the twenty-sixth be convenient?

EP: Yes, that will be great.

GA: See you then. Do you have all your ROs (repair orders) so I can review what's been done to date?

EP: Yes, I do, I keep all materials about the car and its servicing.

GA: Good. . . . That will make it much easier to follow the history of the problem.

11

■

Public Utilities

■

STATEMENT OF PHILOSOPHY

Public utilities are virtual monopolies—at least in your home area where you usually have scant choice as to brand selection. But despite how large and powerful and daunting they may be, utilities are very likely to offer you a favorable settlement. The one proviso is you have to be tenacious—if you don't give in first, chances are they will.

• After a lifelong love affair with his city, Scott D. became disenchanted with the impossibly high cost of living and moved his family to the suburbs. He missed the city terribly, and all his regret coalesced into one relatively trivial circumstance: For the life of him, Scott could not understand or accept the fact that his electricity bill was three times higher than it had been in the city.

In a misguided effort to confront the issue, he became obsessive about saving electricity, to the point that he insisted members of his family figure out what they wanted before they opened the refrigerator door, because he claimed that browsing its contents wasted electricity. That the electric bills remained high only exacerbated his mania.

Scott also called the electric company frequently, lost his composure, made accusations about the incompetence of the meter readers, and generally earned himself a reputation with the customer service department of being a nut case. Representatives seemed to enjoy telling him his bill, though very high, was consistent with what it had been for the previous owner.

Three years passed. Then, when Scott's neighbor moved and the big house next door remained vacant for some months, the electricity bill correspondingly plummeted. Scott knew it had to be more than coincidence: A little investigating turned up the fact that his neighbor had been tapping into their line.

Scott took the matter up with the power company, but because he had not kept records of the events, and was also less than a popular customer, he failed to get the immediate cooperation his problem deserved. Instead of pressing for a refund on the obvious overcharge, Scott counted his blessings and took the reduced charges as victory enough.

• Seizing upon a suddenly available opportunity to rent in a better neighborhood for less money, Gail G. moved her fancy specialty shop from one part of the city to another. Her cat-quick, midnight move required a change in phone numbers, which didn't matter to Gail as long as the phone company played a message on her old number telling callers about her new number.

Naturally, however, there was a screw-up: Not only was telephone service at her new place delayed for ten days, but the message on her old number said, "Disconnected at customer's request." Without a forwarding number, and with no new line in service, Gail's customers assumed she'd either flaked out, gotten into some mysterious trouble, or gone out of business.

Weeks later, Gail accidentally learned about the costly screw-up. However, because the situation was a bit complicated, she was unable to persuade any of the customer service reps she spoke to that the phone company had made a mistake that entitled her to some compensation. To her few returning customers she said, "Whaddaya gonna do? It's part of the cost of doing business in this crazy city."

• Larry and Teri K. got married, moved to a new apartment, and called the phone company to arrange for service. They specified to the service representative that they wanted the works—call waiting, call forwarding, speed dialing. They were quoted a monthly fee, installation charges, and given a set date for the installation. On the first set date, Teri stayed home from work and the installer failed to show; Larry stayed home for the second no-show; the third time was the charm.

Already annoyed, they became even more so when their basic monthly charges proved higher than the quote they both remembered. But when they called to inquire, the billing rep told them they must have "misunderstood" the sales agent. Since they didn't know the name of the agent, nor the exact amount he'd quoted them, nor the cost breakdown of their service package, they didn't pursue the issue any further.

• Tirelessly supporting herself with two jobs while attending night school, Carol D. was fiercely proud about holding her own. This included diligently paying her bills on time. Since checking accounts cost money, she paid everything by money order.

When her local phone company notified her that they had not received payment of her last bill, Carol called between shifts and, perhaps overvigorously, explained that she had indeed sent a money order. The customer service rep was less than sympathetic. Carol was told that unless she hand-carried payment to a nearby payment center the next day, her service would be interrupted and a reconnection fee and a $250 deposit would be required.

The words were like a blow; Carol hung up and took a few minutes to gather herself. She knew she couldn't prove the existence of the money order and she didn't have the money to pay the bill a second time. As for the $250 deposit, they might as well have asked her to fork over the Hope Diamond. For months she lived without a phone, a deprivation she responded to in her usual gritty manner by saying, "When the going gets tough, the tough get disconnected."

Utilities are fundamentally different from other industries in a couple of ways. First, what they sell are considered to be necessities of life, not mere life enhancements. Second, there is little, if any, choice about which ones to use. (There are three major long-distance telephone companies, but at the local level no choice exists.) Because of the necessity and monopolistic nature of utilities, many consumers feel at their mercy. The hostility toward utility companies is great, a hostility almost matched by subservience and docility.

Typically, there are four categories of problems that consumers face routinely with regard to utilities: 1. Overcharges; 2. Breakdown or unusability of service without compensation; 3. Unjust deposits for maintaining or reissuing service; 4. Difficulty in obtaining satisfactory service, including noncompensated waiting periods.

I've had substantial experience handling every type of problem with utilities. What I've found is that there are ten rules which, if scrupulously followed, will turn those giant money suckers into the manageable necessities they are supposed to be.

1.   Check all monthly statements carefully. If you find irregularities, or have any questions, call them immediately.

2.   Keep an ongoing Fact Form file of all contacts with the different utilities, for whatever problems you encounter with them. You'll often find later on that one problem relates, unbeknownst to you, to a new problem. Knowing the history of your relationship puts history on your side.

3.   When ordering a new service, or changing an old one, keep the names of all company representatives with whom you have contact. Jot down the order number they assign to your account. This becomes significant if the wrong service is installed or you are billed incorrectly and want to prove the error lies with the utility. Often the utility won't do a full check, and is much more likely to give you the benefit of the doubt if you have your facts.

4.   Never assume the first rep you talk to has all the appropriate information. As with medical opinions, get a second one when dealing with utilities. This is because the options and types of services they offer vary so greatly.

5.   Be tenacious. In pursuing a problem, you must be prepared to outlast them. Due to their sheer size, they employ hundreds, if not thousands, of people in customer service capacities. Accumulate facts, build your power base, then when you reach the individual who is compelled by your well-documented, unemotional approach and authorized to give you resolve, you will usually win.

6.   Pursue a supervisor right off the bat. The knowledge and helpfulness of low-level reps is wildly uneven. I don't know how many times I've heard an array of contradictory stories. Besides, supervisors are much more vulnerable and responsive to pressure points. (On occasion, merely pressing for a supervisor will coax an entry-level rep to take action on your behalf.)

7.   Handle problems in this area by telephone. But be sure to document every verbal agreement with a letter of confirma-

tion. The number of problems they handle, the size of the staffs, the frequency of staff changes—any of these can cause decisions made in your favor to get lost in the shuffle.

8.   If you do not make progress using the action plan to get resolve, contact the President's Hotline, a service offered by many utilities aimed at handling problems that haven't been taken care of through ordinary channels.

9.   As a pressure point of last resort, mention that you feel it incumbent upon you to contact the Public Service Commission. (They are located in your state's capital.) All utilities are regulated by state laws and are subject to public hearings. Every time you contact the PSC in your state, a record is kept of your issue. The cumulative information is compiled for use when the utility is seeking a rate hike or other changes in its way of doing business. But do not say, "I guess I'm going to have to go to the Public Service Commission and see what they'll have to say about this." Utilities are highly sensitive about keeping a clean nose vis-à-vis the PSC. Simply say, "Do you think it would be a good idea for me to run this issue by a higher authority?" as a good beginning. If there's no movement, follow up with, "I guess reporting this problem in well-documented detail to the Public Service Commission is the next logical step, don't you think?" Nonthreatening—i.e., disguised—threats pack a lot of wallop.

10.   If you still haven't gotten what you think you deserve, contact the PSC (see chapter 17).

The true-life stories that appear at the beginning of this chapter are a bit quirky—intentionally so. I've had a lot of interaction with utilities, but one story that stands out is itself a bit quirky. Quirky because I was guilty of not following so many of my own rules. When I finally did get into gear, however, good things happened.

As part of the breakup of AT&T, I, like millions of consumers, was given the opportunity to buy the phones I had been renting or else return them and purchase new ones from the phone stores that were popping up all over town. I opted to buy my two phones from the phone company. That was in 1983. Then, in early 1989, I realized while reviewing my monthly charges that I had somehow never questioned my being billed for an "investment recovery charge." Thinking about it, it dawned on me that this phrase was nothing more than confusing language for an ongoing monthly rental fee for the two phones I had purchased six years earlier. Apparently the phone companies had failed to communicate perfectly to each other.

I set about collecting what facts I could, many of which were not in my possession because I'd thrown out the old phones and the receipts for them long ago. I could clearly identify the problem—an obvious overcharge, dating back to 1983—and the desired solution—full refund of back charges, plus interest. I called the billing office of my local telephone company (using the number provided at the top of my bill) and immediately asked to speak to a supervisor, explaining that my problem was very complicated and would save everybody time and energy if I only had to describe it once.

Put through to a supervisor, I told my story, got sympathy, but was told that unless I could prove I'd purchased the phones, no credit could be given. What constituted proof? Either the phones themselves, which had identifiable code numbers, or the sales receipts from 1983. I said I could provide neither one. But I asked if I could please speak to the senior supervisor. You've been very helpful, I said, and I'm sure you wouldn't be satisfied with a "no action possible" response if you were in my shoes and had overpaid $150 or so. (Creating empathy, talking person-to-person, human being to human being, is always an effective and affecting tactic.)

I was put in touch with a Ms. Pride, who listened to my story and suggested I get someone at AT&T to check the records. If my story was confirmed, she would "consider" credit. I thanked her and contacted AT&T's customer service 800 number that Ms. Pride had given me. I asked to please be connected to a supervisor who had specific experience with "investment recovery charges." Instantly recognizing my preparedness, they directed me to a Mr. Jameson, who, without hesitation, accessed my records and saw that no recovery charge was applicable to my account.

However, I didn't think my word alone would be enough for Ms. Pride. Nor did I want to wait for Mr. Jameson to contact her in writing, knowing that delays open the window for the strangest eventualities. So I asked Mr. Jameson if he had conference-calling capabilities, and he said yes. He located Ms. Pride at the billing office, the issue was quickly resolved, and she said she'd call the next day to tell me the exact credit amount. I, in turn, got their addresses, in order to be able to write them confirmational letters. On my next month's bill I received a credit for $158.34.

PORTNOY'S FACT FORM (SIDE ONE)

Step 1. Product or Service Information
Telephone Company
Tel. no. 555-1234

Step 2. Problem Statement
Billing error 1983–1989 (to date)
Ongoing charge for "investment recovery charge." Local company claims I rented phones that I bought outright in 1983 from AT&T.

Step 3. Desired Solution
Credit for 6–7 years of billing overcharges, plus interest

Step 5. Actual Solution/Confirmation Communication–Date
Credit received in the amount of 158.34.
Confirmation letters sent to:
  Ms. Julie Pride, 1/15/89
  Mr. Paul Jameson, 1/15/89

PORTNOY'S FACT FORM (SIDE TWO)

Step 4. Name/Contact	Title/Company	Comments/Action/Date
Patricia Ellenson	Customer Service rep., local phone office	Put in contact with Evelyn Smith.
Evelyn Smith	Supervisor, local phone office	1/14/89; wants proof of purchase; puts me in contact with Julie Pride.
Julie Pride	Senior Supervisor, local phone office	1/14/89; for credit needs AT&T confirmation— suggests calling AT&T business office at 1-800-555-2000; ask for supervisor knowledgeable about investment recovery charge.
Paul Jameson	Senior Supervisor	Obtained confirmation; contacted Ms. Pride via conference call; credit agreed upon; she will call me on 1/15/89 to indicate the amount.

SAMPLE FOLLOW-UP CONVERSATION
WITH THE TELEPHONE COMPANY

STEP ONE:
Contact local telephone business office; number listed on monthly bill.

TC: Good afternoon. Customer service, Patricia Ellenson.

Get to a supervisor!

EP: Yes, hello, Ms. Ellenson. I have a very complicated billing problem. May I please be connected to a supervisor so time and energy can be saved for everyone.

TC: What is your telephone number?

EP: 212-555-1123.

TC: Please hold.

TC: Evelyn Smith.

EP: Hello, Ms. Smith. My name is Eli Portnoy. My telephone number is 555-1123. I have noticed what I think might be a problem on my January bill. The problem goes back to 1983. I hope you can assist me with it.

TC: Let me bring your account up on the computer. . . . Now what seems to be the problem?

When you are not sure, ask. People love to offer explanations and advice.

EP: Can you explain the monthly investment recovery charge on my bill?

TC: This is a monthly fee we collect for your nationwide telephone service based on the phones you are renting from them and have been renting since 1983.

EP: Ms. Smith, I thought there was a problem. I do not rent any phones. When AT&T split up, I was given the opportunity to buy my phones, which I did.

TC: Well, our records do not show this. Do you have any records to prove you actually bought the phones?

EP: What would constitute proof?

TC: The phones themselves have code numbers; or the sales receipts.

EP: Unfortunately, I do not. I replaced those phones two or three years ago.

TC: Mr. Portnoy, I'm afraid unless you can substantiate your claim, I cannot help you.

Be tenacious! Create empathy! Take the corporate player out of her usual role.

EP: Ms. Smith, we have to be able to come up with some solution. What would you do if you were overcharged for six years for something you don't even have? I appreciate your help, and I'm sure you wouldn't be any more satisfied than I am. If you were sitting in my place, and were owed as much as $150, what would you do?

TC: I sympathize with your problem, Mr. Portnoy. I don't know if anyone can help you, but let me put you in touch with someone who might be able to. Hold on please . . .

TC: Mr. Portnoy, this is Julie Pride. I am the senior supervisor at this business office. Ms. Smith has briefly explained your problem. Would you fill me in please?

[I related the story again.]

Tell your story as many times as you need to, briefly, concisely, clearly, unemotionally.

TC: Mr. Portnoy, the only way I could see you obtaining a credit considering the circumstances is if someone at AT&T could check your records and confirm what you told me. Then I'd consider authorizing credit.

Always thank people for their assistance. Courtesy goes a long way. Also, get whatever information you need for the next step.

EP: I'll try that right now, Ms. Pride. Thank you so much for your help. Do you have AT&T's number for this kind of information?

TC: Yes, you can call 800-555-2000.

EP: And if I need to reach you again, how can I do so directly?

You've made an ally; make sure you have access to them again.

TC: Just call the number you called before and ask for me.

EP: Thank you again, Ms. Pride.

AT: May I help you?

Get to the heart of the matter in order to get right to someone who can handle your problem.

EP: Yes, a senior supervisor at my local telephone business office, Ms. Julie Pride, referred me to you to resolve a billing error that dates back to 1983. Could you connect me with someone who is knowledgeable and familiar with the investment recovery charge please.

AT: Let me check.

AT: Paul Jameson, may I help you?

Always indicate who referred you.

EP: Hello Mr. Jameson. My name is Eli Portnoy, telephone number 212-555-1123. I have just been referred by the senior supervisor of my local phone company's business office, a Ms. Pride, to resolve the billing of an investment recovery charge to my account since 1983. In fact, I bought my phones at that time, but in order to receive credit for this obvious overcharge, I must be able to prove it. Can you pull up my records dating back to 1983?

Tell your story and update the problem, i.e., you need proof.

AT: Let me get your records. Please hold. . . . Yes, Mr. Portnoy, there is no reason why you should have had the investment recovery charge on your bill. It was a mix-up that occurred during the breakup.

You don't want delays. Try to get the player to act directly on your behalf. If necessary, create more empathy and press for help.

EP: Mr. Jameson, is there some way you can contact Ms. Pride at the local telephone company and convey this information to her? Do you have conferencing capabilities?

AT: Yes, I do.

AT: Ms. Pride, this is Paul Jameson at AT&T. Mr. Eli Portnoy is on the line with us. I am calling in regard to the investment recovery charge Mr. Portnoy has been paying since 1983. Our records show this billing is improper.

TC: AT&T doesn't have any record of rental phones since March of 1983 for Mr. Portnoy?

AT: No, we don't. He should be credited fully for the past years.

TC: Fine. Mr. Portnoy, let me call you tomorrow with the exact amount of the credit. And sorry for the mistake.

Get addresses for confirmation letters or thank-you notes.

EP: That's fine, and thank you both. Before you get off the line, may I have your office addresses? I would like to send letters of confirmation to you both.

1/15/89

Mr. Paul Jameson
Senior Supervisor
AT&T
123 1st Street
East Orange, NJ 23083

Re: Investment Recovery Charge Overbilling: E. Portnoy, 212-555-1123

Dear Mr. Jameson:

As per our conversation in conference with Ms. Julie Pride, senior supervisor at the local telephone company, this letter is to confirm that I will receive a full credit in the amount of $158.34 to offset incorrect billing relating to the investment recovery charge from 1983 to date.

Thank you ever so much for your help in resolving this matter.

Sincerely,

Eli Portnoy

[An identical letter was sent to Ms. Pride.]

▪ ▪ ▪

Many consumers are having problems with the interactive telephone services. The numbers related to these services offer conversation with strangers, live sex talk, or sex talk on tape. The dismay of parents whose children use these numbers is a well-documented issue. Less well known is the fact that because these numbers are not regulated as to price, they can change suddenly and astronomically: A number advertised as costing $1 for the first minute can, a short time later, cost $100 for one minute. If you want to use these numbers, it is a very good idea to find out what the current charges are before you make the call. But if you do get burned, the phone company will intercede on your behalf and strike the charges from your bill. In order to have them do so, follow the action plan just as you would in handling any other problem.

The one difference in the situation is that the phone company will ask you whether you want those numbers blocked—i.e., you won't be able to call them from your phone. If you say no, and then try to get them to strike the charges a second time, your likelihood of succeeding will be greatly reduced. So, if you make a mistake, or someone else uses your phone to call one of those numbers without your approval, take action. Many states as of this writing are considering enacting laws to restrict access to these telephone numbers.

▪ ▪ ▪

12

Retailers, Mail Order, Banks

RETAILERS

Oftentimes there is no problem with the product itself;
the problem is with the retailer in the form of overcharges, billing errors, store return policies, a missing
credit or refund for merchandise returned, false guarantees, or goods ordered and paid for but not received.

• Mark S., an executive with a sporting-goods company, had
to buy a baby gift for a business associate whose wife had just
given birth. Not knowing the associate well, Mark went to a
well-known baby-oriented store so the new parents would be
aware he'd spent a nice piece of change, and in the event they
didn't like the gift, it could be easily returned.

As luck would have it, he bought the same sterling silver cup two other people gave them. They laughed about it, and the associate suggested he exchange it for a sterling rattle. But the store didn't carry sterling rattles and they wouldn't offer a refund, only a store credit. What am I going to do with a store credit at a baby-gift shop? he wondered. Taking the cup, he went elsewhere to buy the rattle. The cup sat in his closet—and is probably still there.

• Jason L., a financial analyst, was a very thorough shopper, one who checked out all the facts and prices related to a purchase before buying. After researching the marketplace, he decided on a particular VCR, and went shopping for the best price. Finding what he thought was the best deal, he bought the VCR at a store whose advertising guaranteed that its prices were the lowest available.

A week later Jason saw the same VCR for $65 less. Thinking, "What a bonus, a certain refund," he returned to the store where he'd bought his VCR. The salesman, then another salesman, and finally the manager refused to honor his claim. One after another, they simply said they couldn't authorize a refund at this point in time. There was a little scene, Jason left without satisfaction, and the experience ruined the pleasure he'd gotten from his "smart shopping."

• Bill G. and his wife, Marcia, spent weeks looking for new furniture for their new house. Eventually they found exactly what they wanted at a place they never expected to find it—a major department store. They paid by credit card, and were told they wouldn't be billed until the merchandise actually left the warehouse.

Six months later the furniture had yet to arrive, but the bill appeared on their monthly statement as of month three. When a dunning notice appeared on their next bill, they were furious. Marcia called the store and asked to speak to their salesman, but he no longer worked at the store. The department manager told her the merchandise had just gone out, and she should go ahead and pay the bill. This she did.

Again they waited. And again, no furniture. Marcia called the store, got the manager, and was told he had made a mistake—the furniture was still not on its way. "What is going on here?" Marcia exploded. The manager's attitude made her madder and madder. "Cancel the whole thing," she said. The manager told her they would have to forfeit one-third of the total bill because the order was a special one, which was the reason for the absurd delay. "No one told us any of this," Marcia protested. But the manager was obstinate. Thinking she had taken a wrong turn into the Twilight Zone of shopping, Marcia agreed to the forfeiture. And that wasn't the end of it either. The department store reported them as a credit problem for delinquent payment on the furniture. "Will we be hounded by this for the rest of our lives?" Marcia asked Bill.

There are a few laws that govern retailers that every consumer should be aware of. (The law may vary from state to state, but only slightly.) In the first place, every retailer is obligated to refund a customer's store credit if no purchase has been charged against that credit at the end of a six-month period. (Thus, Mark S. could have waited and gotten a refund from the baby-gift shop.) Secondly, unless store policy explicitly indicates otherwise at the point of sale, retailers are obligated to convert the credit into cash if the customer has not used the credit within a six-month period.

However, if a retailer clearly posts a sign at the cash register or at some other conspicuous spot stating the store's policy— Store credit only for returns; No exchanges after seven days; Cash refunds with receipt only within ten days of purchase, etc.—then the customer is considered legally forewarned and must abide by the policy.

This leads us to a few fundamental rules every consumer should follow when buying retail:

1.   Always find out exactly what the store's return policy is in advance of making a purchase. If necessary, consult store personnel.

2.   Pay by credit card whenever possible to ensure protection via the Fair Credit Billing Act. Had Bill and Marcia presented a well-documented case to their credit card issuer, they would almost certainly have gotten all their money refunded.

3.   When dealing with a retailer, use the face-to-face method whenever possible. The retailer wants to see the merchandise and ascertain that it is in the same condition as when sold.

4.   Get the names of everyone you deal with.

5.   If you plan on being a regular customer or are considering making an expensive purchase, it is a good idea to introduce yourself to the manager and/or the owner. Even a small encounter may be the difference in their waiving a store policy on your behalf.

Several years ago I bought a new TV. I had shopped the market for a couple of weeks, and settled on a top-brand, large-screen stereo model. I bought it from a retailer who advertised that they were never undersold.

A few days after making the purchase, I ran across an ad for the same TV selling for $150 less. I put together my facts, problem statement and desired solution, got a copy of one of the retailer's advertisements, plus my original bill of sale, and went back to my retailer.

My salesman responded to my presentation by denying the legitimacy of the advertisement. I sought out the store manager, but he was not available. The assistant manager and I then had a discussion about the legitimacy of the ad. I was unemotional and courteous throughout—yet he would not concede the point. He told me to take up the discussion with the store's manager, a Mr. Fuentes.

I noted all these facts on my Fact Form, then called the store's executive offices. (I got the number by calling directory assistance.) I asked for the name of the person in charge of retail personnel. This turned out to be a Mr. Soto, a name I knew might come in handy as leverage later.

The next day I called Mr. Fuentes, briefly outlined my story, and asked to meet with him. He begrudgingly agreed, but only after I asked him whether he'd rather I try to get the problem resolved through the store's corporate offices. "Which," I said, "I'd be glad to do if you don't have the authority to okay the refund I'm entitled to."

We met that evening. I told my story again, showed the competitive ad, and presented my original bill. He asked whether I'd tried to buy the item for the price in the ad, and I said no, because I'd already bought it from his store, which guaranteed they offered the lowest prices in town.

He stood fast, claiming there was no proof the other price was a valid one. I told him in that case his ads should specify that they would honor other prices only if positive proof could be provided. And what would that proof be? I asked. Then I asked him what he would do if he were in my shoes? How would you handle this? He was getting flustered, and said he didn't know.

Then I asked for the proper spelling of his last name and his exact title. Why? he asked. I didn't threaten, I simply and calmly said that I was surprised, given his store's prominent ad campaign and success, that he would go to certain lengths to avoid honoring the store's avowed commitment to their customers. Thus, I felt compelled to contact his superior—Mr.

Soto—to find out why the company's policy had changed. I said I understood his position, but that I thought mine would be understood by Mr. Soto.

Suddenly, he asked to see my documents again, motioned me to the cash register, and immediately authorized a credit for $150.

This case shows that if you're in the right, gain just a little bit of leverage, and stand your ground, you'll get what you deserve.

PORTNOY'S FACT FORM (SIDE ONE)

Step 1. Product or Service Information
Electro Brand 25″ Stereo TV, Model 2500
Purchased from Cheap Sam's Electronics, 222 8th Ave. New York, NY
cost: $525; price guaranteed as lowest
Purchase date: 4/8/87

Step 2. Problem Statement
Competitor's ad for same product $375 (4/11/87).
Cheap Sam's won't meet lower price by refunding differential.

Step 3. Desired Solution
Refund of $150

Step 5. Actual Solution/Confirmation Communication–Date
Received refund of $150; 4/14/87

PORTNOY'S FACT FORM (SIDE TWO)

Step 4. Name/Contact	Title/Company	Comments/Action/Date
Sal Giordano	Salesman, Cheap Sam's	4/12/87; questioned legitimacy of ad.
Robert Klein	Assistant Manager, Cheap Sam's	4/12/87; questioned ad. Suggested I contact Mr. Fuentes, Manager.
Mr. Soto	Head of Personnel, Corporate Executive Offices—555-6000	4/13/87; got his name from operator to use as leverage, if necessary
Mr. Fuentes	Manager, Cheap Sam's	4/14/87; met at the store; used Soto's name, credit refund authorized at location.

■ ■ ■

The Fair Credit Billing Act applies to department store credit cards as well as bank-issued credit cards. Needless to say, however, when the retailer and the card issuer are one in the same, the consumer has considerably less leverage.

Take the example of Liza B., who was billed many times for charges made on her upscale department store credit card. She had reported the card stolen and tried many times by letter to persuade the department store that the charges had no business being billed to her account. Then, because the department store had listed her account as delinquent with a number of credit bureaus, her applications for other credit cards were being rejected.

The whole situation was becoming a big bummer. Then a friend alerted her to the existence of the Bankcard Holders of America, a nonprofit consumer group that her friend said had had terrific success mediating disputes between its members and their creditors. Liza joined, and within weeks the unfair charges on her account were wiped out and she was able to get the credit cards that had previously been denied her. (To join the BHA, write 460 Spring Park Place, Suite 1000, Herndon, VA 22070; membership is $18 per year.)

The Fair Credit Reporting Act is another excellent consumer protection. Under the FCRA, consumers can write directly to credit bureaus (retailers, by law, must supply the names of the bureaus) and demand that they be able to review their credit reports. If you have been denied credit within the last thirty days, the review costs nothing. In any event, the credit bureau itself is bound to investigate your allegations and, if it finds in your favor, must send a corrected report to any party that has been influenced by a negative report.

▪ ▪ ▪

MAIL ORDER (THE DIRECT-MAIL INDUSTRY)

If a problem arises with a mail-order company, a simple phone call to the customer services/relations department will almost always resolve the issue.

• Roberta C., a saleswoman for a housewares company, traveled nearly three hundred days a year. To save time, she became an avid buyer of clothes through mail-order catalogues. Once, she ordered a summer dress from the catalogue of a well-known West Coast direct-mail company. She paid by credit card. When the item arrived, it not only didn't fit properly but, as far as she was concerned, bore zero resemblance to the photograph that had enticed her to buy it. She decided to return it as soon as she returned from her business trip.

In the meantime, she got her credit card bill, and not thinking twice about it, paid it in full. She figured they'd give her a credit when she returned the dress.

She followed the return instructions to the letter. The instructions made no mention of a specific carrier or a need for a return receipt. To her surprise, there was no credit applied to her next bill. She called the customer service department, and they were very nice, but had absolutely no record of the return and so couldn't responsibly offer credit. She explained her end of the situation, but the company said the burden of proof was on her. Having no idea what to do, Roberta simply let the matter drop.

Roberta had indeed reached the point of no return; she had made so many mistakes that all she could really do was learn from the experience. As regards unhappiness with items purchased by mail order, there are a few hard-and-fast rules.

With your merchandise, mail-order companies generally send along a form for you to fill out and instructions for merchandise returns and credits. Regardless of how those instructions read, return the merchandise via a service that provides a receipt stating that the company received the item. If the item cost what you consider to be a lot of money, insure it.

Another problem consumers run into with mail-order companies is that they don't get what they ordered. It is important to remember that federal law requires direct-mail retailers to refund a customer's money no later than eight weeks after the merchandise has been ordered and not sent. Many companies will send you a letter asking if you wish to continue waiting for the back-ordered item. You decide. If you paid by credit card—which you should if you can—the transaction cannot be charged until the merchandise is ready for shipment.

If merchandise has been delayed beyond eight weeks and the company has not contacted you, and your efforts to contact them have not met with an acceptable response, get in touch with the Federal Trade Commission, Division of Enforcement, 601 Pennsylvania Avenue, NW, Washington, DC 20580; or call 202-326-2996.

Also, if you have any problem and aren't getting satisfaction, a letter detailing one's experience should be sent to the Mail-Order Action Line (6 East 43 Street, New York, NY 10017). They will intercede on your behalf with the mail-order company in question.

If, however, you feel you've been the victim of mail-order

fraud (federal prosecutors say it is the safest crime to get away with, and the hardest to prosecute), contact your local Postmaster, the Chief Postal Inspector, U.S. Postal Service (Washington, DC 20260-2100; or call 202-268-4267) and your local Better Business Bureau.

As the following story shows, paying by credit card is the best hedge against unexpected problems.

I arranged to send a gift to a client from an established direct-mail food company. I paid by credit card for second-day delivery. I clearly identified the address to which the basket of food was to be sent.

Four days later I called the client to see if the food had arrived—it had not. I called the direct-mail company's customer service department, got the original order operator—whose name I had jotted down—and determined that she had written the address down incorrectly. She assured me the order was traceable and the merchandise would arrive the next day. It did not.

When it did arrive, five days later, the food was crushed and unappetizing. I called the company and requested a refund, based on the fact that the food did not arrive on time and was not in condition to be consumed. The company, for reasons I could not understand, would only authorize a credit for the special shipping costs. Three days later I received a call from the mail-order outfit stating that I should take my problem up with the shipper.

I waited until my credit card bill arrived, then wrote a letter following my standard procedures of documentation—the facts relating to the purchase were outlined, a problem statement was delivered, and a desired solution was stated (full credit for the food and shipping). I sent the letter to my card issuer; they investigated, and two weeks later I received full credit.

PORTNOY'S FACT FORM (SIDE ONE)

Step 1. Product or Service Information
Juicy Foods, San Ysidro, CA, tel. no. 800-222-6662
Purchased $85 basket to be sent to Tom L. at 16 West Park
Road, Arlington, Va. 22102
Paid $15 for second-day delivery—meaning 6/10/89
Operator: Ellen Huss

Step 2. Problem Statement
Address taken incorrectly; 6/14/89 hadn't arrived; given assurances that it would arrive the next day. Arrived 6/18/89
in no condition to be eaten; crushed.

Step 3. Desired Solution
Full refund of $85 + $15 = $100

Step 5. Actual Solution/Confirmation Communication–Date
Credit card company confirmed full credit—$100, 7/1/89.

PORTNOY'S FACT FORM (SIDE TWO)

Step 4. Name/Contact	Title/Company	Comments/Action/Date
Ellen Huss	800 number operator; 222-6662	4/10/89; took incorrect address
Alan Bendel	Customer Relations Rep.	6/18/89; won't authorize credit, except for special shipping costs. Says I should take the matter up with the shipper.
Customer Service Dept.	credit card company	6/18/89; wrote letter detailing situation, asking them to take my case.

BANKS

For years, banks have been notorious for being less than helpful to individual consumers. Indeed, many banks have withdrawn from the retail end of the business altogether, claiming it isn't sufficiently profitable. Considering the attitude, it is a good idea to go and meet and greet your bank manager, no matter how small a depositor you are.

• Kenny A., a warehouse manager for a toy manufacturer, had banked with the same bank for ten years. He received a notice from his bank saying he was overdrawn, and that the check for his rent had bounced. Kenny knew the bank had made an error, and he had a bad relationship with his landlord, who was always looking for some reason to get him out. He called the bank's customer service department (he didn't know the bank manager), described what was happening, and was told that he was indeed overdrawn. He transferred money to his checking account from his savings account to cover the check in the event his landlord tried to redeposit.

When Kenny received his monthly statement, he noticed that a check he had written for $355 was listed as being for $855. He called the bank again, and was told to send a copy of the check along with a letter explaining the situation. Two weeks later he received a letter from the bank, which passed off all responsibility onto others. Meanwhile, his landlord was processing for eviction. Kenny needed a letter indicating he had no responsibility for the trouble. When the bank refused, he seethed.

Besides knowing the bank manager, who might have been more helpful, Kenny should have tried to conduct all his banking business on-site, at the bank. Banking problems are best resolved in person during the middle of the morning or the early afternoon.

If you have a banking problem and are unable to resolve it using the action plan, take all your documents, put them together, and write your state banking department, located in the state capital. If that fails, contact the Federal Reserve Board, Division of Consumer and Community Affairs (Federal Reserve Board, Washington, DC 20551). If your bank is not part of the federal reserve system, contact the Federal Deposit Insurance Corporation, Office of Consumer Affairs (550 17 St., NW, Washington, DC 20429; or call 800-424-5488).

For national banks, contact one of their district offices for the comptroller of the currency (located in New York, Atlanta, Dallas, San Francisco, Kansas City, and Chicago). For federally chartered savings and loans, contact the Federal Home Loan and Bank Board, Office of Community Investments, Division of Community Affairs (1700 G St., NW, Washington, DC 20552).

But, as always, when you have a problem, even a discouraging one, pursue resolve by going into action with the action plan. Here is an example of a banking story that proves the point:

A check I received from one of my largest clients bounced. It was possible, but extremely unlikely, that this company would bounce a check. In turn, my bank notified me that two checks I had written to pay suppliers had also bounced. I was angry and embarrassed. Immediately I set out to get a new check from the client, or get the money wired into my account. If it was a banking error, I desired to obtain an apology and, more importantly, corresponding letters of apology sent to my affected suppliers.

I collected all my facts on the Fact Form. Wanting to

determine exactly what had gone wrong, I contacted my client and the banks involved. My client assured me the check was good. He gave me the name of his company's personal banker to contact. My own banker said he had to look into it and would call me back. When he did, he told me the check had been submitted for payment to the originating bank and been rejected for an improper signature. (This was not unusual, but in this case it was odd because the corporate check was signed with a legitimate stamp signature used by companies that write numerous checks a day.) My banker told me to get another check from my client; he could not follow up with the other bank, nor could he help me out vis-à-vis apologizing to my suppliers. That's the responsibility of the other bank, he said.

I called Mr. Ross, the banker my client had referred me to. He said he knew nothing about the problem, but was sure it wasn't his bank's fault. (How he could be so sure was a total mystery.) His advice to me was also unsatisfactory. Realizing that he was one of many VPs with little authority or desire to resolve my problem, I decided to pursue a higher authority—in this case the bank president's office. I intended to use the secretary to the president tactic described in chapter 6.

I told my story in full to the president's secretary, including the story of the cavalier manner of VP Ross. The next day she called me and said the bank would wire the appropriate funds to my account, and that if I would give her the names and addresses of my suppliers, she would have the bank apologize in writing to them. As for Mr. Ross, someone would be in touch with him concerning his deportment and approach to my problem.

PORTNOY'S FACT FORM (SIDE ONE)

Step 1. Product or Service Information
1) $10,000 check from MLS Marketing Company drawn on Bank of Chicago, Michigan Avenue Branch, Account no. 952431625. Date: 6/3/88. Address: 901 Michigan Ave., Chicago, IL.
2) $1,500 check from Portnoy & Co. to Ganzer Graphics drawn on New York Federal, Fifth Avenue Branch, Account no. 222356789. Date: 6/6/88. Address: 12 East 40th St., NYC.
3) $750 check from Portnoy & Co. to Rapid Printers drawn on New York Federal, 5th Ave Branch, Acct. no. 222356789. Date: 6/6/88. Address: 40 Houston St., NYC.

Step 2. Problem Statement
$10,000 check bounced from MLS account, 6/5/88.
$1,500 and $750 written on the $10,000 sum bounced as a result, 6/8/88.

Step 3. Desired Solution
New check from client, or funds wired from client's bank directly into my account as quickly as possible

Step 5. Actual Solution/Confirmation Communication–Date
Money wired into my account 6/13/88.
Apology letters sent to my clients. They redeposit their checks.

PORTNOY'S FACT FORM (SIDE TWO)

Step 4. Name/Contact	Title/Company	Comments/Action/Date
Ron Jacobs, client	VP, Marketing, MLS Inc.	Check is good. Banker is Mr. Ross. Will supply new check but takes a week to 10 days. Contact Mr. Ross and clients accounts payable dept. 6/10 telephone call.
Paul Rolof	Manager, NY Federal (my banker)	Check signature "supposedly" improper—check rejected. Suggests contacting client's bank to pursue new check from foul-up at client's bank with inspection clerk. He talked with Alice Ensen of Bank of Chicago on 6/10.
Peter Ross	VP, Corporate Accts., Bank of Chicago	Ross states that bounced check is not his bank's fault; contradicts my banker's information. Suggests redeposit and "wait and see—it will resolve itself." Will get back to me. Spoke to him 6/10.
Mrs. Thompson	Executive Secretary to President, Bank of Chicago	Thompson will check facts. Will contact Ensen and Ross and get back to me next day. 6/12 call.
		Thompson concurs with facts. Error corrected, fault of Bank of Chicago. Money to be wired to my account ASAP. Apology letters to be sent to my suppliers and my bank. Mr. Ross's action to be reviewed internally.

13
.
Consumer Products

■

STATEMENT OF PHILOSOPHY

If you have a problem with a product and pursue resolve with the action plan at the retail level without getting results, do not give up. Take your case directly to the manufacturer. If you stick to the action plan with the manufacturer, an overwhelming percentage of problems will be resolved in your favor.

• Anne H., a free-lance writer who depended on her answering machine as a lifeline to her livelihood, purchased a new machine that stopped taking messages within three weeks. The outgoing message would play to the caller, but the incoming communication was not being recorded. She had bought the machine from one of the largest discount electronics retailers, and the machine itself was manufactured by a well-known company.

Anne took the machine back and showed it to the original salesman. He referred her to the service department. They agreed to look it over and, as the unit was still under its ninety-day warranty, said repair would be free and quick. When she picked it up a week later, the service department said they had had no difficulty making the repair.

Two days later the machine acted up again. Twice more she brought it back for repair, but each time the problem reoccurred. It was already much more trouble than it was worth. She presented her case to the store manager, asking for a replacement. He refused. "You got a lemon, it happens," he said. "Don't bother with the manufacturer," he advised, "that'll just be a pain. Get a new machine and chalk it up to bad luck." She did.

• David H. got a CD player from his wife for his birthday. He hooked it up to his state-of-the-art sound system and settled back, expecting the clearest listening experience of his life. To his surprise, however, after a while there would be whole passages of music that blurred. Then the sound would return to its crystalline perfection. He tried a variety of CDs, but the blurring occurred each time. He took the player back to the audio store, and strangely enough, the symptom couldn't be reproduced during the few minutes the machine was tested, first by the salesman, then by the serviceman, and finally by the manager. Baffled, David took it home, only to have the same experience. This time he returned to the store and in a determined fashion insisted that some employee listen to the machine until the problem showed up. "I don't have all day, sir," was the common reply. The store manager refused to replace the item, claiming that if the sound quality was erratic at home, it must be on account of some dysfunction in his other equipment. Terribly frustrated, David decided maybe the new technology was not for him.

• Kate L. loved coffee, espresso, cappuccino. For ten years she brewed her coffee in a simple drip coffee maker, and only had espresso and cappuccino when she went out. Then, as a reward for a promotion at work, she decided to get herself a new top-of-the-line combination coffee/espresso/cappuccino maker. The machine cost well over $200 and for the first three months functioned wonderfully. Suddenly, though, it started making mild coffee and too-weak espresso and cappuccino. She took the machine in for repair. Although it was no longer under warranty, the store agreed to fix it for a minimum fee of $50. It didn't seem right to her to spend so much on something, only to have to throw more money at it soon after purchase. Yet, she thought, what's my option? She paid the $50, and the retailer came back with the infuriating conclusion that the machine was not reparable, that she must have used it improperly at home. Kate was too mad to think straight. She bought another inexpensive drip coffee maker, and gave up the at-home pleasures of espresso and cappuccino.

• John H. bought a lot of shoes from a well-known American company, famous for their classic styling, comfort, and quality finish. The shoes were very expensive, but John always rationalized that they lasted a long time. "Besides," he liked to joke, "a centipede like me shouldn't pinch when it comes to footwear." Then he bought a pair of tan loafers made by the same company from a major department store that had represented the line for many years. Of course he got them in his usual size, trying them on before buying them.

Oddly, after wearing them twice, he decided they were distinctly tighter fitting than any other size nines of this same brand. He returned to the store and explained the oddity to the salesman. The salesman, and then the department manager, implied that the problem might be in his mind. "But even so," said the manager, "if you hadn't already worn them outside, and they weren't showing any marks, I'd be happy to give you a new pair in the next size." The long and the short of it was, tough luck.

When John suggested he'd take the matter up with the shoe manufacturer, the manager said fine, but don't expect any help from them. "They stand by their goods through thick and thin. We've had a lot of trouble dealing with them over the years." John was discouraged from pursuing the matter further. A year later he went back to the store to make a scene after finding out that the manager had just been feeding him a line—the shoemaker was, in fact, famous for satisfying its customers.

Problems with consumer products are notoriously plentiful. Either products are defective from the outset, malfunction after a brief period of time, fall way short of expectations, or resist all efforts at repair.

The point of this chapter is to remind you that if you encounter any problem with a consumer product, follow the action plan at the retail level. And if you get stonewalled at every level of retail authority, then pursue resolve through the manufacturer. Chapters 6 and 7 on phoning and letter writing explain in detail exactly how to identify and locate the manufacturer, how to get in touch with the right people, and how to proceed with your case up the corporate ladder.

Because you can never predict whether a retailer will behave honorably, you must never allow them to discourage or dissuade you from taking your case straight to the manufacturer. Sometimes a retailer will try to cajole you with all sorts of friendly, sympathetic banter intended to restrain you from contacting the maker of the product. Don't fall for anything.

When approached, according to the rules of the action plan, manufacturers are generally responsive. They'll send a corporate technician to your home who'll either fix the problem or authorize replacement; or they'll put pressure on the retailer to treat you fairly; or they'll resolve the matter in your favor in some other manner.

I have resolved hundreds of problems with consumer products. The one that comes to mind is significant because I had to use all the tools in combination in order to achieve the results I knew I was entitled to. It was also an especially interesting case because of the amount of time that elapsed between the time of purchase and the final resolve in my favor.

Two and a half years ago I purchased a new stove-top/oven for my home, one that had a built-in grill and removable cooking cartridges. It was manufactured by a company that heavily advertises the quality, durability, and custom features of its products. After a few months, however, several problems appeared: The oven temperature was much lower than the indicator reading; one of the two original stove-top cartridges malfunctioned; and cooking times could not be accurately anticipated. A repairman from the retailer came to my home, made some minor adjustments to the thermostat, and replaced the malfunctioning cartridge. The new cartridge lasted barely three months. Seven times over the next year and a half servicemen came to fix the appliance, which, in one way or another, seemed to be more on the blink than usable. Each time, temporary positive results were achieved, only increasing my frustration. I kept a record of each visit, noting the exact nature of each repair.

Then, when the left stove-top cartridge began to work only on the "high" setting, I decided to bypass the retailer, who had been extremely cooperative (which was the reason I hadn't bypassed him earlier), and contacted the manufacturer. The customer service department reacted to my presentation promptly. They sent a regional distributor's serviceman who attempted to fix the appliance, but failed. Then they sent a corporate technical service person who, after evaluating the problem history, concluded a total unit replacement was in order. The replacement was confirmed by the director of customer relations over the phone, and I, naturally, confirmed our verbal agreement by writing a letter of confirmation. My letter outlined the oven's history, the regional distributor's efforts, and the recommendation of the corporate service adviser. A brand-new unit was delivered and installed by the regional distributor, who told me to contact him immediately if I ever encountered any other problems with products he was responsible for.

PORTNOY'S FACT FORM (SIDE ONE)

Step 1. Product or Service Information
Modern Cook Oven/Stove-Top Combination
Model 2000
Serial # 2672542A

Step 2. Problem Statement
1) Oven temperature lower than central knob reading.
2) Stove-top cartridge temperature malfunction. Works on "high" setting only.
3) Cartridge replacement (11/19/88) malfunctioned as well.

Step 3. Desired Solution
Repair (satisfactorily) or replacement of total unit

Step 5. Actual Solution/Confirmation Communication—Date
Unit replaced 12/10/88 by authority of manufacturer.
Delivered and installed by L&R Appliances, regional distributor, 12/21/88.

PORTNOY'S FACT FORM (SIDE TWO)

Step 4. Name/Contact	Title/Company	Comments/Action/Date
Ed Biondo	Salesman, J&R Appliances (555-2432)	Invites me to visit appliance store 5/21/87 to review proper appliance operation. Result: I was using it properly. Repairman sent 5/22/87. Repaired. (Steve Plaino)
" "	" "	Repairman sent 2/2/88. Repaired. (Dave Molinski)
" "	" "	Repairman sent 5/12/88. Repaired. (Dave Molinski)
" "	" "	Repairman sent 8/29/88. Repaired. (Dick Simmons)
" "	" "	Repairman sent 9/20/88. Repaired. (Dick Simmons)
Erik Landers	Director, Customer Service, Modern Cook, Inc. (305-555-2222)	J&R Appliances, the regional distributor, sent Peter Brooks, technician. Unit was evaluated, cartridge replaced, oven repaired.
" "	" "	Corporate technician sent. Total unit replacement, 12/21/88.

SAMPLE TELEPHONE FOLLOW-UP
THE CLINCHING CONVERSATION

STEP ONE:
Check owner's manual for manufacturer's address and telephone number.

STEP TWO:
Call 800 information to determine if a toll-free number applies, after you have determined location. If not, call the local telephone information service for the manufacturer.

Always ask for customer service.

MC: Modern Cook.

EP: Yes, Operator, what is the name of the director of customer service?

MC: Erik Landers.

EP: Thank you. Could you connect me, please.

MC: Customer service.

EP: Erik Landers, please.

MC: Who is calling?

"Leverage" your referral to avoid cold reception by company.

EP: Eli Portnoy. I am a customer who has been referred to Mr. Landers to resolve my problem.

MC: Mr. Landers' office, this is Debbie Justin.

EP: Ms. Justin, my name is Eli Portnoy. I have been referred to

Mr. Landers to assist me in my efforts to resolve a series of problems I am having with my Modern Cook unit.

MC: Have you spoken with your retailer yet?

EP: Yes, extensively and without satisfaction. That is why I am calling Mr. Landers.

MC: One moment, please.

MC: Landers.

State your problem clearly, concisely. Stay to your facts!

EP: Yes, Mr. Landers, this is Eli Portnoy. I purchased a Modern Cook oven/stove-top combination unit, model 2000, in April 1987. Since delivery I have had to have the temperature control system adjusted five times by J and R Appliances, the retailer from whom I originally purchased the unit in New York City. The problem has continued on and off for a year and a half. In addition, one of the stove-top cartridges is now malfunctioning, working on only low and high and no in-between settings.

Identify your desired action/solution.

I am calling to arrange for a corporate technician to evaluate my equipment and to determine if it is reparable or should be replaced by you, the manufacturer.

MC: Mr. Portnoy, what have the appliance repair people told you is wrong or has been wrong with the unit?

Stay on target with your facts and objective: This corporate player can help you.

EP: In each case, they have told me "nothing major" is wrong, but they have made minor fine-tuning adjustments on each visit. At the end of each visit the unit works to their satisfaction and they depart. I continue to feel the temperature settings do not match the actual temperature in the oven. This has significantly affected my family's cooking results.

MC: I see, yes, I would imagine it would. Mr. Portnoy, I would like to arrange for our regional distributor, L and R Distributors, to send one of their factory-trained technicians to your home to check it out. Would this be satisfactory?

All right. The facts are getting you results.

EP: Yes, it would.

MC: Good, I will have them contact you later today. When can they best reach you?

Obtain direct follow-up info, in case things "fall through the cracks" at corporate end.

EP: Anytime today. My number is 212-555-1234. By the way, what is their number in case I miss their call?

MC: 718-555-6000; they are located in Queens, New York.

Later That Day

Corporate follow-up from distributor as promised: good first sign.

L&R: Mr. Portnoy, this is Peter Brooks, from L and R Distributors. I have been contacted by Mr. Landers at Modern Cook to come and see your malfunctioning oven.

EP: Yes, Mr. Brooks, thank you for following up. Can you come tomorrow?

L&R: How about Wednesday, late afternoon? Will someone be home?

EP: Yes, I will make sure of it.

Two Weeks Later

If you need additional help, quickly remind the corporate person of your previous interaction and thanks for his/her attention to your issue.

EP: Mr. Landers, this is Eli Portnoy. You arranged for L and R Distributors' technical service person to check my oven two weeks ago. Thank you for your prompt attention to my problem.

MC: Yes, I remember. How did things work out?

EP: Unfortunately, the service work performed did not resolve the problem and the new stove cartridge I purchased from the distributor is heating only on low and high, not in between.

MC: Mr. Portnoy, L and R couldn't repair the unit?

State your case and restate your resolve along with your facts. Create empathy.

EP: No, they repaired it, but within the week the inconsistent heating problem reoccurred. Mr. Landers, I think at this point I would like a new unit, since not even your distributor's technical people can fix the problem. Plus, the cartridge isn't working properly either and it's brand-new.

MC: Mr. Portnoy, I am sorry for the continued problem. If you would permit me, I would like to send one of our corporate people to look at the unit. Is that satisfactory?

Be clear what you want when asked.

EP: Yes, it is under the condition that if it is determined to be irreparable, you will agree to replace the unit with a new one at no charge. You realize this has been going on for eighteen-plus months.

MC: Let me get this person's evaluation and I will consider replacement if it is warranted. If you can hold a moment, I will see if I can get him on the line and arrange an appointment. . . . Mr. Portnoy, how is next Saturday morning?

EP: That's fine.

MC: I will call you after he has inspected the unit.

Always get follow-up information. You'll never know when you need it or wish to use if for thank-yous or confirmation of agreements.

EP: Thank you, Mr. Landers. May I have your business address for my files? . . .

Monday

MC: Mr. Portnoy, this is Erik Landers, from Modern Cook.

EP: Yes, what are the results? Your man was here for two hours Saturday.

You Win!

MC: After reviewing the technician's evaluation and the repair history you sent me, I am pleased to offer you a replacement unit at no cost. No one can quite figure out the problem with your unit. I am arranging for L and R Distributors to deliver and install a new unit next week. Will that be okay?

Remember to be appreciative. Politeness counts a lot.

EP: Yes, indeed. That's terrific. Many thanks for following through for me on this problem.

12/2/88

Mr. Erik Landers
Director, Customer Service
Modern Cook Inc.
120 Water Street
Maple Shade, NJ 23083

Re: Oven/Stove-Top Model 2000: Continuing Repair Problems

Dear Mr. Landers:

As per our telephone conversation yesterday, this letter confirms that a Modern Cook corporate service technician will come to my home to evaluate the ongoing temperature control problem I am having with my Modern Cook unit, model 2000, purchased from J and R Appliances, New York City, in April 1987. Further, I have outlined below the service history of this unit as further evidence of the long-standing mechanical problems I have experienced with this unit.

After you have reviewed the technician's evaluation and this history, I hope you will be able to authorize a no-cost replacement unit.

Date Purchased:	4/20/87	
Serviced by J&R:	5/22/87	(Steve Plaino, Repairman)
Serviced by J&R:	2/2/88	(Dave Molinski)
Serviced by J&R:	5/12/88	(Dave Molinski)
Serviced by J&R:	8/29/88	(Dick Simmons)
Serviced by J&R:	9/20/88	(Dick Simmons)
Serviced by L&R Distributors:	11/19/88	(Peter Brooks)

If you have any questions, please give me a call. I can be contacted during the day at 212-555-1234.

I look forward to a successful resolution of this problem.

Sincerely,

J. Elias Portnoy

12/24/88

Mr. Erik Landers
Director, Customer Service
Modern Cook, Inc.
120 Water Street
Maple Shade, NJ 23083

Re: Replacement Unit Model 2000 for Portnoy

Dear Mr. Landers:

Thank you for your efforts on my behalf and your agreement to replace my Modern Cook oven/stove-top unit at no cost.

As I understand it, L and R Distributors will contact me to arrange for delivery and installation of the new unit.

I am very pleased that Modern Cook stands behind its products and look forward to uneventful use of my new unit.

Sincerely,

J. Elias Portnoy

■ ■ ■

If using the action plan at the retail level and then with the manufacturer still does not bring satisfactory results, contact the Major Appliance Consumer Action Panel (MACAP, 20 North Wacker Drive, Chicago, IL 60606). This independent consumer group is composed of industry experts and will mediate problems with manufacturers. Contact them in writing, using the same procedures outlined in the letter-writing chapter. Deliver your facts, problem statement, and desired solution, and include copies of sales receipts, repair orders, and any correspondences.

But remember: Use MACAP (and indeed any higher authority) only as a last resort. Before you actually use them, mention to the stubborn director of customer relations that you are going to. Do not threaten! Simply say, "If you were me, would you think that my next logical step would be to present my case to MACAP?" Sometimes this last-ditch nudge stimulates action.

■ ■ ■

14

■

Personal Services

■

STATEMENT OF PHILOSOPHY

The personal services area is perhaps the most difficult in which to get resolve through the utilization of the action plan. Disputes are often based on quite subjective issues. When the issue is tangible and clear-cut, however, the action plan is still far and away your best bet for getting what you deserve.

• Russell P. hired a pest control company to rid his house of the fleas his two dogs had brought in during the spring. He was careful to tell the sales representative over the phone that it was imperative that whatever substance or solution the company used, they would have to take into account the presence of his two-year-old daughter and highly allergic wife. The pest person assured Russell that they would not be using a toxic mix, and that the house would be totally habitable within one hour after the spraying.

As it turned out, though, the potency of the spray was so intense that when Russell and his family returned to their home many hours after the stated time, both his daughter and wife became ill. The family was forced to move to a hotel for two nights until the toxicity subsided. The spray had indeed killed the fleas, but Russell felt he should be compensated for the expense of the hotel stay. He paid his bill, then tried to argue his case—to no avail.

• Joe and Sally G. decided to build an extra bedroom and bath on their Cape-style house to accommodate the arrival of their second child. They asked their friends for recommendations of contractors. Three gave them the names of companies whom they had used successfully. Joe went with the lowest bidder, J and L Construction. The contractor seemed affable and knowledgeable. The job was to take six months. A year later, with the newborn sharing tight quarters with mom, dad, and sis, work had stopped and the contractor, who was nowhere to be found, had more of their money than Joe and Sally had of a completed renovation.

In general, problems in the personal services area are best handled *beforehand*. There is nothing like the existence of a specific, complete contract, detailing exactly what work is expected, as a hedge against problems. Drawing up an appropriate contract is easy: Simply follow the same rules you follow when filling out your Fact Form. State clearly and concisely what it is you are paying for. Then have both parties sign and date it, and if possible, you keep the original. If a personal-services company balks at this arrangement, it might be a good idea to look for another company.

Another form of leverage that consumers have in the personal services area is that in many cases the service is provided prior to the transfer of payment. Thus, if you review the work and find that it does not meet with your approval, withhold payment—at least until the situation is rectified to your satisfaction.

But, in cases where you've paid in advance, or paid a substantial deposit, or paid periodically, or been unhappy with some consequence of the service, go into action. Proceed up the ladder until you reach the person—oftentimes the owner—who has the authority to give you the resolve you deserve. If the work hasn't gone the way it should have, or if some damage has occurred along the way, include a photograph of the problem. Indicate to the appropriate person that you will be sending them a letter with a photograph. Photographic documentation in cases where damage has ensued is very persuasive.

Here is an example of just such a case:

I hired a well-known, well-advertised refinishing company to sand and stain my living room floors. I called the company and arranged for an on-site visit and estimate. Everything went smoothly. The estimate came to $450, and I paid a $200 deposit. Because the odor would be awful for a couple of days, I stayed across town with friends.

When I returned, the floors looked great. But I also noticed that the frame of the antique mirror on my wall had been totally cracked, as if it had been dropped to the floor. No one tried to contact me about it, nor was there any note of explanation. I took out a Fact Form and decided to do a little information gathering. After three calls, I determined what the frame was most likely worth, and how much repairing it would probably cost. Without this information, I couldn't very well deliver a problem statement, let alone a desired solution. The mirror was worth $1000, and the cost of repair was $300 to $400.

I called the sales agent with whom I had contracted for the floor work. He denied any knowledge of the incident, but said he would check with the men who did the job. I asked for the name of the company's owner—"so I can send him documentation." "Sam Reston," he begrudgingly revealed. I didn't wait. I took a photograph of the damaged frame and called the owner at his office.

Mr. Reston said no one had mentioned the problem to him, but he would look into it. I told him I would send him a letter detailing all the facts and enclose a picture of the damage. Further, I said, since I had already paid a deposit of $200, and the damage was going to cost me anywhere from $300 to $400, I would go by the lower figure in order to be fair, which meant that the company owed me $50. I repeated that I would document everything in writing.

Within a week after sending the letter with a photograph, Mr. Reston messengered me a check for $50.

PORTNOY'S FACT FORM (SIDE ONE)

Step 1. Product or Service Information
Manhattan Floor Refinishing Service
$450 Estimate to sand and stain living room/entry area floors
$200 deposit given on 5/5

Step 2. Problem Statement
Frame of $1000 antique mirror severely cracked during work on floor.
Repair estimate: $300–$400

Step 3. Desired Solution
Reimbursement for damages. Willing to settle for difference between money owed—$250—and lower estimate of repair—$300: $50

Step 5. Actual Solution/Confirmation Communication–Date
Received check for $50, 5/20/88

PORTNOY'S FACT FORM (SIDE TWO)

Step 4. Name/Contact	Title/Company	Comments/Action/Date
Brian Elliot	Sales Manager, Manhattan Floor	Contacted by phone (555-4321) on 5/11/88. Said he had no knowledge, would check with workman and get back to me.
Sam Reston	Owner, Manhattan Floor	Contacted by phone (555-4321) on 5/13/88. Unaware of problem, will look into it. Sent letter and photograph documenting incident and detailing my position, 5/13/88.

5/13/88

Sam Reston
President
Manhattan Floor Refinishing Service
222 East 96 Street
New York, NY 10023

Re: Mirror Frame Damage, Portnoy Residence, 5/11/88

Dear Mr. Reston:

Thank you for taking my telephone call yesterday. As we discussed, although the refinishing work on my apartment's living room and entry area floors is well done, an antique mirror frame in the living room was accidentally cracked while the workmen were working in the apartment.

The estimate for the total refinishing job was $450, of which I paid you a deposit in the amount of $200 on 5/5. The balance due is $250. The estimate to repair the mirror is $300 (estimate attached). I have also enclosed a photograph of the damaged frame for your review. If you need to see the frame damage in person, please give me a call.

I would appreciate receiving a check from you for $50 to cover the difference between the balance due and the repair cost.

If you have any questions, I can be reached at 212-555-1234.

I look forward to hearing from you.

Sincerely,

J. Elias Portnoy

■ ■ ■

When doing work on your home a plethora of problems can arise. Poor workmanship, shoddy materials, schedules that are woefully unmet and inconveniencing, and work that just isn't completed to your satisfaction are among the most typical troubles. Although the action plan may very well get you resolve from a home-improvement company, the best idea is to make sure a solid contract is drawn up before the work begins. Oral agreements about what is going to be done are just so much air; vague, abbreviated descriptions of the work to be done are not really any more binding. If you don't want to use a lawyer, use the same guidelines for drawing up your own contract that you apply to filling out your Fact Form. Be clear. Be specific. Be complete. Doing so will save you all sorts of headaches later on.

It should also be noted that a few remodelers offer warranties under the Home Owners Warranty Program (2000 L St., NW, Washington, DC 20036). To find out which remodelers make this offering, write them. Also, the Better Business Bureaus in Chicago (312-444-1188), Cincinnati (513-421-3015), Columbus (614-221-6336), Lubbock, TX (806-763-0459), Oklahoma City (405-239-6081), Philadelphia (215-496-1000), and Pittsburgh (412-456-2700) will give you the names of remodelers who have agreed to let arbitrators decide disputes.

If you don't have a contract, and there is no local arbitrator, try a local consumer agency like the Better Business Bureau. On occasion, merely bringing a problem to their attention and notifying the contractor of such action will rouse the remodeler to action on your behalf. In cases in which you can identify and prove fraud, contacting your state's attorney general's consumer affairs office may prove effective.

At least four states—Arizona, Hawaii, Maryland, and Virginia—and one locality, Suffolk, New York, have set up "recovery funds" that reimburse a consumer who can prove he or she was victimized by a licensed contractor. These funds are financed by contractor licensing fees. Mechanics for payment vary. Contact each state department of consumer protection for specifics.

Additional guidelines to consider in advance of selecting a contractor:

1) Determine if the contractor is licensed. If so, check with your local municipality's building department to confirm the contractor's "good or bad" standing with the town based on prior complaints. (Saving money by going with an unlicensed company can be a costly headache down the road.)*

2) Contact your local Better Business Bureau office to see if anyone has filed complaints about your prospective contractor.

▪ ▪ ▪

If a dry cleaner ruins a piece of your clothing, present your case in the usual unemotional, brief way. But if you've failed using that method, your local consumer agency or Better Business Bureau will send your gar-

---

*New York City's consumer affairs commissioner announced in early 1990 that under New York state law if an unlicensed contractor brings suit against a consumer for nonpayment (based on the consumer's dissatisfaction with work done), the courts will side with the consumer because the proprietor is unlicensed. This ruling has far-reaching effects that could relate to any unlicensed business that a consumer contracts for work. Check with your attorney general's office to see if laws in your home state are consistent with those in New York. A note of caution: Consumers who do not have documented reasons for nonpayment will be unlikely to receive such a favorable ruling.

ment to the International Fabricare Institute, located in Silver Springs, Maryland. The IFI has eleven thousand member dry cleaners for which it analyzes clothing and mediates disputes. If the IFI finds that the dry cleaner is at fault, they will almost surely pay up. If the garment has been mislabeled, however (if it says "dry-clean" when it should say "hand wash"), use the action plan to pursue the garment's manufacturer. Include a copy of the IFI report in your letter and ask for a refund.

If nothing is working, this is the only instance where I suggest staging a minor public-relations stunt. Wait until there are a number of customers inside the dry cleaners, then go in and make your case forcefully, showing the problem garment and possibly raising your voice a little. Dry cleaners depend so much on local goodwill, they might be moved to resolve your issue without further muss or fuss.

▪ ▪ ▪

Travel agents or tour operators cannot be made to stand by subjective descriptions. If the sparkling beach actually looks bleak, if the lively entertainment puts you to sleep, who's to say whether it's a matter of perception or reality?

If, on the other hand, there has been obvious misrepresentation—the room called the deluxe suite is really closet-sized; the absolute quiet is in truth a noisy major construction site—then you might get help. The U.S. Tour Operators Association (211 E. 51 St., New York, NY 10022) and the American Society of Travel Agents (1101 King St., Alexandria, VA 22314) each have hundreds of travel-agent and tour-operator members, all of which have agreed to submit to mediation by them.

Of course, if you've been the victim of outright fraud—there's no hotel or no plane, and you have to pay a second time—call your attorney general's office or consumer protection. They will combine with law-enforcement officials to try to find the dishonest agent.

▪ ▪ ▪

15
.
Airlines, Rental Cars, Hotels

■

STATEMENT OF PHILOSOPHY

We're told we live in a service economy—well, serve this. It's more like a disservice economy—at least that's how it feels too often. Problems with airlines, rental cars, and hotels abound. Fortunately, the vast majority of them are susceptible to the action plan.

• Robert S. and his wife were on vacation in Mexico. At the airport on the day they were scheduled to return home, they learned that their first flight segment had been canceled, and no other flights were available or scheduled through Mexico City, their connecting city. They were offered two choices: Stay an extra day (which meant missing work and having to pay for a hotel—a cost they were not assured they would get back), or pay $550 extra and take a different route entirely. In either case they were still flying on an American carrier, yet when they reached their destination, the customer service person they approached acted like the problem was endemic to Mexico and had nothing to do with the airline.

• Gary G., a manager for an industrial supplies company, rented a full-sized American sedan from a rental car agency in Denver. He'd opted for the larger, more expensive car because he had a lot of highway driving in front of him. Twenty-five miles down the road, he realized that the car's steering wheel was shimmying badly. The car was difficult, not to say dangerous, to drive above 40 MPH. It wasn't feasible to call the rental agency and wait for an exchange to arrive, so he just drove painfully slow the whole trip.

When he returned the car, he described the problem he had had to the check-in agent. What can you do for me considering the inconvenience, he wanted to know. We'll take the car out of circulation and fix it, he was told. This was not what Gary had in mind. He inquired about some compensation, but the agent said no, since he had been able to get where he was going; the fact that he didn't get there comfortably or on time was just one of those unfortunate things. Gary wanted to "unfortunate" him through the wall.

• Paul M. arrived in Cleveland after a day of meetings in two other cities and a long, delayed flight. Arriving at his hotel, he was told his room was not quite ready and that he could relax for a few minutes in the lounge until it was. Three hours passed before he finally demanded a room from the clerk at the front desk. Assigned a room, he was appalled at its condition. Besides everything else, the sink was dripping noisily. Calling the front desk, he growled, "I've got a room that looks like an ashtray, and a sink that leaks with better water pressure than some states get."

Eventually the room was cleaned and the sink fixed. But the hotel offered no compensation, and Paul was incensed that he had to pay so much for so little. "If I'd been paying for trouble, I definitely got my money's worth," he said later.

Consumers face a nice variety of problems when it comes to the travel service area. With airlines, there's lost luggage, delayed flights, canceled flights, missed flights, reservations not honored, overbooking, and property or physical damage (food poisoning, ailments caused by in-flight conditions). With rental cars, there's reservations not honored, overcharges, rate irregularities, defective cars, and unavailable models. With hotels, there's reservations not honored, overcharges, rate irregularities, unclean rooms, unacceptable service in public areas, and burglaries.

Then there's rudeness, indifference, incompetence, and attitudinizing. Add it all up and it's likely you haven't always felt well treated.

The bright side is that in this area, the action plan is most effective. When presented with a well-documented case of their shortcomings or abuses, service companies tend to respond decently. Of course, you have to be prepared to go right up the ladder—from the site of your trouble on to corporate if necessary. (If your problem occurred in New York and the company's headquarters is anywhere else in the United States, remember: Bypass the New York City office and go straight to corporate.)

In this area one case of mine stands out because it involved all three tools, was especially complex, and would have been a terrible load on my mind if I hadn't gotten sufficient compensation.

I went to Los Angeles on an important business trip. The trip was a disaster. Meetings were missed, phone calls weren't returned, everything was out of sync. When I returned to New York, I found out that the reason for all my trouble was an inadequate message service at the Holmes Hotel where I'd stayed. Messages that were key to the success of my trip simply never got to me. Instead of solidifying contacts and writing new business, the trip had actually cost me in angry clients and missed opportunities.

I collected my facts: The dates of my stay at the hotel; the number of my room; the circumstances of my trip; the names of the people who tried to contact me; and the approximate times of their calls. I called the hotel and asked to be connected to the manager. He was not available. I spoke with the assistant manager, who said he would look into the matter and discuss it with his manager, Mr. Richards. He said he would call me back. I didn't wait. I put all my facts together in a letter to the manager. I said, in effect, that as a business traveler I could not afford to stay in a hotel whose failure to provide basic service disrupted my business and, in essence, cost me money. As compensation, I said I would accept either a full refund on the cost of my three-day stay or, in the event he intended to remedy the message service problem, I'd accept a free equivalent length of stay at some future point.

The manager responded immediately to my letter. Over the phone he said he was very sorry for my trouble and deeply grateful to me for providing the kind of feedback he needed to run the hotel properly. Based on my facts he had conducted an investigation and found that the entire staff of operators routinely turned the buzzers off that signal them when to get back on the line and take a message. Because of this lazy and unbelievably irresponsible behavior, guests at the hotel hadn't been receiving messages for who knows how long. Yet, the manager assured me, my letter was his first inkling of the problem. He also assured me that he had replaced the operator staff and was personally supervising the new one. Would I please give him the opportunity to demonstrate the improved service by accepting a full week's lodging plus meals anytime within the next year? I accepted his offer and immediately sent a letter of confirmation/thanks.

PORTNOY'S FACT FORM (SIDE ONE)

Step 1. Product or Service Information
Holmes Hotel, Manhattan Beach, California
3/12–3/15
Room 714
Cost: $130 per night

Step 2. Problem Statement
Failed to receive at least 12 calls during 3-day stay. Probably cost me money; wasted my trip. (List calls and times)

Step 3. Desired Solution
Full refund, or if service fixed, equivalent number of days' lodging

Step 5. Actual Solution/Confirmation Communication–Date
Seven days free lodging anytime during coming year; plus meals (est. value $1200).
Sent letter of confirmation/thanks to Mr. Richards on 3/25.

PORTNOY'S FACT FORM (SIDE TWO)

Step 4. Name/Contact	Title/Company	Comments/Action/Date
Robert Simmons	Assistant Manager, Holmes Hotel	3/20; contacted at 714-555-8888. Said he'd contact manager Michael Richards and discuss. Richards will call me back.
Michael Richards	Manager, Holmes Hotel	Contacted by letter on 3/21. He called to express apology on 3/25. Offered 7 days free lodging; I accepted.

SAMPLE TELEPHONE CONVERSATION
HOLMES HOTEL

STEP ONE:
Retreive hotel telephone number from hotel bill.

STEP TWO:
Call hotel manager's office.

HH: Holmes Hotel, Manhattan Beach.

Get the facts and the names of all contacts.

EP: I'd like the manager's office, please—and please tell me, what is the name of the manager?

HH: Michael Richards. I'll connect you.

HH: Executive offices.

EP: Good morning. Michael Richards, please.

If the corporate player you desire is unavailable, determine if his/her immediate subordinate is available and get his/her name.

HH: I'm sorry, Mr. Richards is not available. Can someone else help you?

EP: Is the assistant manager available?

HH: Yes, he is. That's Mr. Simmons.

Tell secretary quick summary of purpose of your call.

EP: May I speak with him? This is Mr. Portnoy. I was a recent guest at your hotel and I have a problem I would like to discuss relative to my stay.

HH: Hold, please. I'll see if he's available.

HH: Robert Simmons.

Tell your story. Only the facts. Service/ Problem/Desired Solution.

EP: Mr. Simmons, my name is Eli Portnoy. I stayed at your hotel for three days, March twelfth through fifteenth in room 714. During my stay, I missed at least twelve telephone messages from business associates who tried unsuccessfully to reach me. I learned this upon my return to New York after I missed the most important meeting I had come to Los Angeles for. I was told that the hotel operators would not come back on the line to take messages if the room did not answer. Are you aware of such a problem?

HH: Mr. Portnoy, no, I am not. This sounds very unusual and unlike our hotel. I will have to look into this with the manager, who is unavailable at the moment. Are you sure about this? We have never had a complaint before about our message service.

Corporate player may not believe you. But remember, you have facts, not hearsay.

EP: Yes, I'm quite sure. I even have many of the calls and callers and times documented.

HH: Oh, I see. Well, let me discuss this with Mr. Richards and I'll have him call you back. What days were you here and in what room?

EP: I was there March twelfth through fifteenth in room 714.

HH: We'll be back to you.

Find out "when" they will get back to you.

EP: When?

HH: As soon as I speak with Mr. Richards and we have a chance to check this out.

EP: Mr. Simmons, would you like the list of calls and times?

HH: No, no, that is not necessary.

EP: I see. Well, I'll expect to hear from you. My number in New York is 212-555-1234.

HH: Okay, good-bye . . .

3/21/87

Michael Richards
Manager
Holmes Manhattan Beach Hotel
14451 Manhattan Beach Blvd.
Manhattan Beach, CA 90254

Re: Hotel Stay 3/12–3/15, Room 714

Dear Mr. Richards:

I spoke with your assistant manager, Mr. Robert Simmons, yesterday, and outlined the difficulties I experienced obtaining telephone messages during my recent stay at the Holmes Hotel in Manhattan Beach.

Specifically, at least twelve attempts that I am aware of were made by business associates to leave messages for me during my three-day stay (3/12–3/15) in room 714. They are documented on the attached sheet. This problem was greatly worsened by the fact that one of those calls caused me to miss the most important meeting I had planned to attend in Los Angeles and nearly cost me that client. It certainly cost me money.

I cannot understand how a hotel like yours that promotes itself as a businessman's hotel can fail to provide the most basic service as message taking to busy, on-the-road, business people like myself. I have had good experiences with the Holmes chain in the past and assume this experience was an exception and not the rule.

I would appreciate it if you would look into this problem immediately. If it continues, not only will I have to find another area hotel for my Los Angeles trips, but so will many other business people. I am sure you understand this concern.

Further, as compensation for my troubles, I would also appreciate receiving a full refund for my stay or an equivalent number of free days' lodging (if the problem is resolved), since I did not receive the full services of the hotel as I was entitled to for the daily room rate I paid.

I look forward to your reply. I can be reached at 212-555-1234 during business hours, and, yes, you can safely leave a message.

Sincerely,

J. Elias Portnoy

Att.

Portnoy; Room 714; Hotel Stay: 3/12–3/15
Missed Business Calls

From	Date	Time
Secretary NY office	3/12	11:50 A.M.
Secretary NY office	3/12	1:45 P.M.
Larry Bast Bast and Associates	3/12	2:30 P.M.
Robert Preston Preston Design	3/12	3:00 P.M.
Secretary NY office	3/12	3:50 P.M.
Jeff Bliss C.C.M.	3/12	4:00 P.M.
Joe Miles, MLS Inc.	3/13	8:30 A.M.
Winston Mark Neutro Corp.	3/13	8:45 A.M.
Secretary NY office	3/13	9:00 A.M.
Lonnie Glazer Glazer Associates	3/13	11:00 A.M.
Donna Sands, MFW	3/13	3:00 P.M.
Secretary NY office	3/14	8:30 A.M.

3/25/87

Michael Richards
Manager
Holmes Manhattan Beach Hotel
14451 Manhattan Beach Blvd.
Manhattan Beach, CA 90254

Re: Seven Days' Free Lodging Voucher for J. E. Portnoy

Dear Mr. Richards:

Thank you for promptly investigating my case concerning the missed telephone messages. I am sorry to hear that you had no other choice but to dismiss most of your operators for deliberately turning off their ring-back switches to avoid taking messages. I'm surprised it took so long for someone to bring this to your attention.

I appreciate your offer and accept your voucher for seven days' free lodging anytime during the coming year. I am pleased you were so responsive to my concerns and found them justifiable.

Thank you again.

Sincerely,

J. Elias Portnoy

▪ ▪ ▪

When dealing with decent-sized companies, there are times when the employee who is speaking with you will genuinely not have any idea whom it would most bene-fit you to talk with. The question "Do you maintain an employee handbook?" is often answered in the affirmative, and gets the person you're speaking with to make a sincere effort to peruse the handbook until he or she has located just the right individual. Along the way, this employee might also mention other names that you should write down and possibly bring into play as leverage later.

▪ ▪ ▪

Denied Boarding on Airlines, e.g., "Overbooking"

Federal regulations require that all domestic airlines with more than sixty seats traveling within the U.S. or overseas must provide remedies to passengers involuntarily denied seating on a flight that they were properly ticketed for and arrived on time for. (This ruling does not apply to inbound international flights on either international or domestic carriers.) The usual procedure is that airlines will first seek volunteers to give up their seats in return for a free ticket or other travel compensation and passage to their destination on another flight. (Note that there are no federal rules governing what incentives the airlines can use for volunteers.) If no volunteers are found, and a passenger is bumped involuntarily, he or she is entitled to the following:

1) Rerouting via another flight within one hour of the original flight's departure time. If this is possible, the airline has no obligation to provide any compensation to the passenger (although many will as a good-faith gesture).

2) If rerouted within one to two hours, the passenger is entitled to 100 percent of the flight cost to their destination, to a maximum of $200.

3) If rerouting requires more than two hours, the passenger is entitled to 200 percent of the flight cost to their destination, to a maximum of $400.

This compensation must be paid either in cash on the spot or by check within twenty-four hours. Further, an involuntarily bumped passenger must receive a copy of these rights in writing from the airline at some point prior to the rerouting.

All other inconveniences that a passenger may experience, including delayed flights and canceled flights, are *not* covered by any federal regulations, regardless of the reason. Airlines may or may not offer incentives or compensation to passengers on a flight-by-flight basis. No set rules apply. That means that if you are delayed three hours due to mechanical difficulties, the airline has no obligation to accommodate you. However, most of the more financially successful carriers generally offer some form of compensation, like meal or drink coupons or, if no other flights are scheduled for that day, gratis hotel accommodations. In the case where no rules apply, use the action plan strategy, stay calm, and negotiate for the best deal you can get.

▪ ▪ ▪

16
·
Resolving Problems with Purchases Made in Other Countries

■

STATEMENT OF PHILOSOPHY

Ever return to the United States dissatisfied with a purchase made on the other side of the world? Or did you fail to obtain the value-added tax that made your purchase abroad worthwhile in the first place? Don't despair. You can take care of the problem right here at home.

• A consultant in the art business, Seymour G., traveled frequently to Europe, where between meetings he liked to shop—especially for clothes. On a trip to Rome, Seymour bought a suit from a famous boutique that bore the name of one of the world's top men's fashion designers. The suit required extensive tailoring, and the salesman convinced Seymour that he should let their expert tailor do the work right there, and then they'd mail the suit along. The tailor, a marvelously flamboyant talker, took exacting measurements. Seymour paid in full and left the shop happy with thoughts about how terrific he was going to look in it at an opening a few weeks hence.

He returned home, and as promised, the suit arrived within ten days. The night of the opening he took out the suit and tried to get into it. Apparently the tailor had confused his measurements with those of someone half his size. The suit was so ill-fitting that his own tailor told him retailoring it would be impossible. Out nearly $1000, Seymour wrote the boutique an angry letter. There was no response. He also went to a local fashionable men's store that carried the designer's line—but didn't get a shred of satisfaction there either. He eventually gave up.

• On her vacation, Sarah J. purchased several pieces of crystal from a well-known factory in northern Europe. The merchandise was way too heavy to carry, but she received assurances that mailing it would be no problem. The factory would even give her a refund for the value-added tax on the spot.

When the crystal finally arrived, all but one piece was broken. Sarah tried to get the U.S. representative for the company to assist her, but he insisted the fault lay with the shipping company. She contacted the shipper, but they vehemently denied any responsibility.

There are cases when using the action plan and contacting the foreign company's U.S. office or retail outlet has produced positive results. What happened to Seymour and Sarah, though, is more common. Many foreign companies actually advise their American outposts not to handle merchandise issues if the merchandise was bought overseas. They cite price differentials and difficulties with accounting in relation to currency exchanges. Others cite the fact that certain merchandise is not sold in the U.S., and therefore would not be resaleable here. A few foreign companies have expressed their position more aggressively: They say they don't want to become "dumping" grounds for unsatisfied American consumers.

Given these constraints, I have found another recourse in the pursuit of resolve. It is based on the theory that Americans themselves may not be universally loved or appreciated in other lands, but as consumers, they are tremendously important to the economy of other countries. It is well known that Americans have a passion for spending money when they travel. Thus, the people tied into tourism and tourist dollars are very sensitive to the negative consequences of well-publicized bad consumer experiences. Whose job is it here in the U.S. to disseminate positive information, plus encourage travel and assist in making arrangements? The answer is: American-based foreign tourist boards.

It is the tourist boards that can be of great assistance in helping you with a problem once you're back in the U.S. Simply applying the action plan to a tourist board, just as one would to a corporation, has achieved excellent results. If there is no tourist board for the country in question in your immediate area, ask a travel agent or call the airline that flew to the country—they will provide you with the address of the nearest one. Using the phone, get the name of a specific person at the tourist board, then write him or her a letter, enclose a copy of your sales receipt, and if possible, a photograph of the problematic merchandise. If what you want is assistance in getting a refund for the value-added tax approach the situation in the same manner, but be sure to be clear in your letter what you are seeking.

A couple of experiences will illustrate the issue:

On a business trip to Europe, I traveled through Denmark, where I bought several household items from a famous design store. The retailer supplied me with the necessary forms to obtain a refund on the value-added tax. The forms are to be exchanged at VAT offices at the country's borders or airports for U.S. dollars. However, the VAT office at the port from which I was departing by hovercraft was closed. I was due $100, which was the amount of money I was going to save by having purchased the merchandise in Denmark instead of at home.

Back home, I put together my Fact Form, then contacted the Danish Tourist Board, first by phone to determine the appropriate person to write to, and then by letter. Three weeks later I received a check from the Danish VAT office at the port from where I'd departed, along with a letter of apology for any inconvenience I might have been caused.

Another story relates to a trip to London, during which I bought a dress shirt from a world-renowned Savile Row tailor. I returned home with the shirt only to discover that it had somehow been damaged. The London tailor did not have a U.S. contact, and the thought of trying to work the issue out by phone or letter seemed improbable—and possibly expensive. Instead, I filled out a Fact Form and contacted the British Tourist Board. I sent them a standard product, problem, and desired solution letter, along with a copy of the sales receipt.

In this case, I didn't want a refund, I wanted an identical shirt. Within four weeks, the tailor sent me the shirt I wanted in perfect condition, accompanied by a letter saying how much he looked forward to my patronage in the future.

In both cases, I sent thank-you notes to the tourist boards, thanking them for their intervention on my behalf.

17
·
Using the Government, Regulatory Agencies, Consumer Groups, and the Media

■
STATEMENT OF PHILOSOPHY

Regarding the use of these higher authorities—the media, government agencies, and consumer groups—there are two caveats: one, always exhaust all possibilities for utilizing the action plan before you resort to outside help—higher authorities are often strained to the maximum and often are unable to get you the quick resolve you're seeking; and two, before you actually enlist the help of a higher authority, mention to the company representative that you are going to contact such-and-such agency, group, or media outlet—this acts as another form of leverage against the company itself.

THE MEDIA

The media, especially local TV stations, have become very involved in presenting consumer causes. There is no doubt that the negative publicity for the offending store or company inherent in these dramas does produce uneasiness, changes in the way business is sometimes conducted, and even specific resolve for certain consumers. However, because thousands of consumer inquiries are received weekly, precious few issues get airtime. Thus, it's best to use the possibility of going to the media as a pressure point—not as a routine means of getting real results.

If your problem is particularly "juicy" or "sexy," hideous or outrageous, the media may be interested. If you do decide to make this contact, pick only one TV consumer troubleshooter or one newspaper editorialist. The industry is small and highly competitive—they require exclusivity. Always use the usual action plan procedures: Clearly outline all the facts, describe your actions plus the reactions to those actions, and attach copies of all relevant documents and correspondences. Put everything in a letter to the consumer reporter, then follow up your letter with a phone call. Mention your letter immediately, then state the problem it describes.

Sometimes, even if the media doesn't publicize your case, they'll respond to good documentation by making a call to the offending company on your behalf. Again, simply notifying the retailer or company in question that you have contacted the media can motivate them to address your problem at the eleventh hour.

Here is an example of how it might work:

Quinn G., a photographer, was due to be married. He scoured the metropolitan area for the right location, and finally selected a restaurant overlooking a magnificent golf course as the site for the reception. In order to secure the restaurant six months in advance, a substantial deposit was made.

Ten days before the wedding, Quinn's mother-in-law-to-be happened to call the restaurant to "check up" on some last-minute details. She was told that the restaurant had been sold the week before, and another affair was scheduled for their day. The new owner said that if they wanted a refund on their deposit, they'd have to take it up with the people who had transacted their agreement.

Desperate to find a substitute location (the refund, she figured, would be addressed later via a lawsuit), she worked as only a mother before a wedding can, and luckily found something suitable in the nick of time. Then, furious at her mistreatment and the rude indifference of the new owner, she dashed off a letter to a TV consumer troubleshooter, and followed up with a phone call. Her desired solution was to "get even" with the new owner—not to mention recoup the $5000 deposit. Although the troubleshooter's producer didn't run the story on the air, one call from her television office to the restaurant resulted in the prompt messengering of a complete refund check.

CONSUMER GROUPS

Consumer groups are private and in many cases funded by members of the respective industries. The most well-known group is the Better Business Bureau. Organized for action at the local city level, you can determine the one best suited for you either by calling your local BBB or by writing to the Council of Better Business Bureaus, Inc. (1515 Wilson Blvd., 3rd Floor, Arlington, VA 22209).

The remainder of this section will outline some especially prominent groups, their functions and locations. If your problem is not covered by one of the following associations or groups, check your public library for *Gale's Encyclopedia of Associations* or the *National Trade and Professional Associations of the United States and Canada*. The other option is to write for the only book I would advise using: the *Consumer's Resource Handbook* (Consumer Information Center, Pueblo, CO 81009). But remember: Before you contact any of these organizations, exhaust all the remedies at your direct disposal. Communication with these groups can take a long time.

BETTER BUSINESS BUREAUS. There are 199 BBBs in the U.S. These nonprofit groups of consumer advocates are supported by industry and corporations. Besides providing advice on how to deal with specific problems, the primary function of the BBBs is to collect data about retailers and companies generated by unhappy consumers, then to disseminate this information in reliability reports. Sometimes it's a good idea to contact your local BBB office and check out a company before you make a purchase. There are no guarantees that anything will come out of a contact with the BBB, but, in general, businesses like to keep their noses clean in relation to them.

BBBs also can offer mediation or arbitration on problems, as long as both parties are willing to participate. (Mediation is an informal attempt to reach a mutually satisfactory resolution; arbitration is more formal—both sides agree to let an independent volunteer review the dispute and render a legally binding decision.)

AUTO LINE. (See chapter 10.) This program, run under the aegis of the BBB, provides mediation of disputes or enlists the aid of qualified community volunteers to resolve dissatisfaction with an auto dealer or nearest manufacturer's rep. They use guidelines set up by the Federal Trade Commission.

Autocap. (See chapter 10.) Five thousand disputes between the auto industry and consumers are mediated each year by the Automotive Consumer Action Panels.

The Center for Auto Safety. A Washington, DC–based group that specializes in providing consumers with information regarding "secret warranties" or free-of-charge repair information that are not announced publicly concerning specific car models. Write to them at: 2001 S Street, NW, Washington DC 20009.

American Society of Travel Agents (1101 King St., Alexandria, VA 22314). This group does well intervening on behalf of the consumer, providing the agent or tour operator is a member.

MACAP (20 North Wacker Drive, Chicago, IL 60606). The Major Appliance Consumer Action Panel will intervene on behalf of consumers in informal mediation. They claim an 80 percent resolution rate in favor of consumers.

National Association of Home Builders. This group is excellent at providing information on how to best handle a dispute if you are unhappy with home remodeling or improvement work done by a contractor. Contact them through the Department of Consumer Affairs, 15th and M Streets, NW, Washington, DC 20005; or call 800-368-5242.

FICAP. The Furniture Industry Consumer's Advisory Panel, supported by the American Furniture Manufacturer's Association, will contact the retailer or manufacturer about your problem. If that fails, they will listen to the case and make a recommendation to the manufacturer—if the manufacturer is one of the association's 375 members. Contact them in writing at P.O. Box HP7, High Point, NC 27261.

THE DIRECT MARKETING ASSOCIATION. DMA helps solve mail-order, telephone-order, or video shopping problems by interceding with companies. Submit all inquiries in writing to Mail-Order Action Line, 6 East 43 Street, New York, NY 10017.

THE DIRECT SELLING ASSOCIATION. This group can be very useful if you think you have been bilked by a door-to-door salesperson. Contact the Code Administrator, Direct Selling Association, 1776 K Street, Suite 600, Washington, DC 20006; or call 202-293-5760.

Of course, there are many other groups. I have restricted this listing to those that are highly accessible and have a high rate of success.

GOVERNMENT AGENCIES

Like the media and consumer groups, government agencies can be extremely helpful—but only as a means of last resort. They're glad to hear from you, but are not always able to resolve your particular problem. The key here is that government agencies are swamped by thousands of requests for help, so many that if time is of the essence, don't bother.

There is one government organization that operates differently—i.e., vigorously and expeditiously: the state *Attorney General's Office.* AGOs are usually located in your state's capital or largest city, or both. Every U.S. state has an AGO, and their consumer affairs and fraud departments can be extremely effective in the pursuit of positive resolve. In addition, just mentioning to an offending company that you (unfortunately) will be forced to contact the Attorney General's Office can stimulate immediate action. Companies as a rule do not like to have their activities brought under scrutiny by the government—especially the AGO. But it is vital to remember that you will be wasting your time if you try to contact them before you've made a full-fledged effort to resolve the problem directly with the company.

In most instances, the AGO will not even follow up on a case that is not extensively documented—even if it's a clear case of fraud. Use the action plan to generate documentation, even if you think there's no hope of success.

A few other government agencies can be helpful:

DEPARTMENT OF MOTOR VEHICLES, CONSUMER COMPLAINTS DIVISION. This agency serves consumers who are unhappy with auto repair, body work, or general auto service. In most states, facilities offering automotive services must be licensed. DMV departments can revoke a license if a certain number of problems are filed against a company in a given period of time. The DMV will also mediate problems between consumers and the auto facility after they have reviewed your case and determined it has merit. All problems must be described in writing, accompanied by copies of all pertinent documents. DMVs are usually headquartered in state capitals.

THE CHIEF POSTAL INSPECTOR OF THE U.S. POSTAL SERVICE. This agency is very interested in consumer purchases made via mail that possibly involve fraud. It can be contacted at the U.S. Postal Service, Washington, DC 20260-2100; or by calling 202-268-4267.

THE FEDERAL TRADE COMMISSION, DIVISION OF ENFORCE-
MENT. This agency will handle problems with merchandise
or mail-order delay. There exist time limits under which direct-
mail companies must deliver merchandise or notify you of your
right to cancel due to delay. They also deal with suspected
irregularities concerning warranties, service contracts, marketing, and advertising. 601 Pennsylvania Ave., NW, Washington, DC 20580; or call 202-326-2996.

U.S. DEPARTMENT OF TRANSPORTATION. This agency will
not resolve individual disputes, but they like to hear about
problems with airlines, and if they hear enough, will force an
airline into compliance. Write: DOT, Office of Consumer
Affairs, U.S. Department of Transportation, 400 7th St., I-25,
SW, Washington, DC 20590; or call 202-366-2220.

THE FEDERAL RESERVE. The Federal Reserve monitors problems with its member banks. First, you must contact the state
banking commission in your home state (usually located in the
state capital). Then, proceed to the Fed. It can be contacted
at the Division of Consumer and Community Affairs, Federal
Reserve Board, Washington, DC 20551. For nonmember
banks, contact the Federal Deposit Insurance Corporation,
Office of Consumer Affairs, 550 17th St., NW, Washington,
DC 20429; or call 800-424-5488.

For national banks, contact one of the district offices for the
Comptroller of the Currency in New York, Atlanta, Dallas,
San Francisco, Kansas City, and Chicago.

For federally chartered savings and loans, contact the Federal Home Loan Bank Board, Office of Community Investment, Division of Community Affairs, 1700 G St., NW,
Washington, DC 20006; or call 202-785-5400.

PUBLIC SERVICE COMMISSION. This agency will handle problems with billing, service, deposit waivers, and anything else you cannot get the utility to resolve. The PSC can check the records of major utility companies by computer; problems can sometimes be resolved quickly over the phone. If a meter visit is required, staffers will attempt to schedule it within two months. The PSC is empowered to order utilities to correct your bill, waive deposit demands, even reimburse you for food spoilage due to electric outages. They are usually located in the state capital.

18
.
A Final Word: Get Leverage and Keep It

■

STATEMENT OF PHILOSOPHY

There are a few simple habits to get into to keep yourself from being stung later on. Once you have found how invigorating—and even fun—it is to resolve a problem by using the action plan, guard against becoming lax and be an educated consumer.

There are seven basic rules to follow that will give you leverage before a problem arises and maximize your chances of winning a case when you're forced to use the action plan.

    1. Get the name of everyone you come into contact with as part of any significant service or product transaction. What at first feels a little unnatural will soon be second nature.

2. At the retail level, if you make a high-ticket purchase, introduce yourself to the store's manager or owner (or both).

3. Always get the return policy in writing, if it isn't clearly stated on your bill, before you pay.

4. Pay by credit card whenever you can. The Fair Credit Billing Act is a potent weapon in your arsenal.

5. If the retailer claims to offer the lowest prices, get the store manager to give you a price guarantee in writing before you purchase the item.

6. Find out what steps the retailer or service merchant will take in the event you are not satisfied. For example, if a contractor is going to do work on your home, get the guarantees established in writing on the company letterhead or stationery or invoice. Have it signed and dated by the manager/owner of the company.

7. Determine where and how a product can be serviced before you make the purchase. If the authorized repair facility is many miles away, you might want to choose a different brand with a more accessible service option. Companies that offer toll-free 800 customer service telephone numbers usually are more interested in your satisfaction than those that do not.

One other slightly different means of getting leverage before a problem arises involves the writing of thank-you notes after someone has helped you resolve a problem. Courtesy is an essential, fundamental element of the action plan. Courtesy, in the form of thank-you notes, disposes the person you've thanked to come to your aid should another problem arise. This is not merely leverage. One thrust of the action plan is to take the emotional and subjective elements out of a problem, while simultaneously humanizing the situation. Instead of an adversarial experience, wherein two beings representing different interests wrangle and tangle, the action plan attempts to bring the consumer experience back to what it really is, first and last—two human beings trying to get along and find resolve.

In the Sixties and early Seventies, people like Ralph Nader acted on behalf of consumers and scored some major successes. His work was, and continues to be, very valuable. But despite how marvelous and hard won these great triumphs have been, things have not really gotten better. In fact, they may very well have gotten worse.

Fellow consumers: The time has come to stop being reactive, to stop taking it on the chin, and in the teeth, and in the pocketbook, from companies. The time has come to be proactive, to make thousands of lightning strikes against companies run by people who are contemptuous of consumers, consumed as they are by their own power, status, and money. Instead of feeling victimized and exploited, tricked and taken advantage of, it's high time to go on the offensive and make ours a consumer-oriented, consumer-driven economy.

If enough of you become proactive and use this book to get what you're entitled to from companies, those companies will be forced to meet their full responsibilities head-on, which, in turn, will enable them to compete in the increasingly competitive global markets of tomorrow. So do yourself, do them, do everybody a favor—Be Proactive.

Index